T0362957

PUBLISHED BY BOOM BOOKS

boombooks.biz

ABOUT THIS SERIES

....But after that, I realised that I knew very little about these parents of mine. They had been born about the start of the Twentieth Century, and they died in 1970 and 1980. For their last 50 years, I was old enough to speak with a bit of sense.

I could have talked to them a lot about their lives. I could have found out about the times they lived in. But I did not. I know almost nothing about them really. Their courtship? Working in the pits? The Lock-out in the Depression? Losing their second child? Being dusted as a miner? The shootings at Rothbury? My uncles killed in the War? Love on the dole? There were hundreds, thousands of questions that I would now like to ask them. But, alas, I can't. It's too late.

Thus, prompted by my guilt, I resolved to write these books. They describe happenings that affected people, real people. The whole series is, to coin a modern phrase, designed to push your buttons, to make you remember and wonder at things forgotten. The books might just let nostalgia see the light of day, so that oldies and youngies will talk about the past and re-discover a heritage otherwise forgotten. Hopefully, they will spark discussions between generations, and foster the asking and answering of questions that should not remain unanswered.

BORN IN 1945?

WHAT ELSE HAPPENED?

RON WILLIAMS

AUSTRALIAN SOCIAL HISTORY

BOOK 7 IN A SERIES OF 35
FROM 1939 to 1973

War Babies Years (1939 to 1945):   7 Titles
Baby Boom Years (1946 to 1960):   15 Titles
Post Boom Years (1961 to 1970):   13 Titles

BOOM, BOOM BABY, BOOM

BORN IN 1945? WHAT ELSE HAPPENED?

Published by Boom Books.
Wickham, NSW, Australia
Web: www.boombooks.biz
Email: email@boombooks.biz

Creator: Williams, Ron, 1934- author.
Title: Born in 1945? : what else happened? / Ron Williams.
ISBN: 9780648651154
Subjects: Australia--History--Miscellanea--20th century.

Cover image: National Archives of Australia.
A9121, L12373A Dame Enid Lyons,
GBE, A1200, L3633 Max Meldrum at work;
A1200, L1136 Children learn to swim;
A1200, L2700 People operating movie projector.

TABLE OF CONTENTS

INTRODUCTION TO THE SERIES

I was five years old when the War started. But even at that early age, I was aware of the dread, and yet excitement, that such an epoch-making event brought to my small coal-mining town. At the start, it was not at all certain that it would affect us at all, but quickly it became obvious that everybody in the nation would become seriously involved in it. The most immediate response I remember was that all the Mums (who still remembered WWI) were worried that their sons and husbands would be taken away and killed. After that, I can remember radio speeches given by Chamberlain, Churchill, Lyons, Menzies, and Curtin telling of hard times ahead, but promising certain victory over our wicked foes.

For a young boy, as the War years went on, reality and fantasy went hand in hand. As I heard of our victories, I day-dreamed of being at the head of our Military forces, throwing grenades and leading bayonet charges. I sank dozens of battleships from my submarine that was always under attack. And I lost count of the squadrons of Messerschmitts that I sent spiralling from the sky. Needless to say, I was awarded a lot of medals and, as I got a bit older, earned the plaudits of quite a few pretty girls.

But, mixed in with all this romance were some more analytical thoughts. Every day, once the battles got going, I would go to the newspapers' maps of where the battlelines currently were. One for the Western front, one in North Africa, and a third in Russia. Later, another in the Pacific. Then I would examine them minutely to see just how far we had moved, backwards or forwards. I read all the reports, true and false, and gloated when it was said we were winning, and shrank away from our losses.

At the personal level, I remember the excitement of getting up at 4am on a few days when nearby Newcastle was under submarine attack. We went to our underground air-raid shelter that we shared with a neighbour, and listened, and occasionally looked out, for some who-knows-what enemies to appear. It really was a bit scary. I can remember too the brown-outs, and the black-outs, the searchlights, the tank-traps, the clackers that were given to wardens to warn of gas attacks, and the gasmasks that 20 town-wardens (only) carried, presumably to save a town of 2,000 people when needed. Then there was the rationing, the shortages of everything, and even the very short shirt-tails that a perceptive Government decreed were necessary to win the War.

At the start of researching this series, everything began to come back to me. Things such as those above, and locations like Dunkirk, Tobruk, El Alemein, Stalingrad, and Normandy. Really, at this stage these names kept popping up, but I was at a loss as to how significant they were. Also, names of people. Hitler and Mussolini I knew were baddies. But **how** bad? Chamberlain was always criticised for his appeasement, but what were his alternatives? Who **were** Ribbentrop and Molotov, and Tojo and Blamey, and what was Vichy France?

And finally, when war did come, and grind on, year after year, what effect did it have back here in Australia? How did we as a society cope with a world that just had to continue on, given that the sons and dads of the nation were actually being killed daily overseas? When the postman did his normal delivery and brought a letter saying your loved one is dead? What did we do when old jobs suddenly disappeared, and new ones were created hundred of miles away? When goods, long readily available, were no longer for sale? When everything changed?

It was all a hotch-potch to me when I started this series. At the end of it, I can say it is a lot clearer. I have sorted out the countable things like battles, locations, people, and rules and regulations. I can appreciate, too, the effects on society, though these can only be ascertained from what I **have** researched, and make no allowance for all that I have missed.

In presenting each war-time book, I have started every chapter with a visit to Europe, and a look at the military events in the world, with increasing emphasis on the Pacific. Then I come back to Oz to see how we are faring in a military sense. After that, I blunder about reporting and speculating on which aspects of life here were affected by these, and other ongoing, matters.

So, despite all the talk about the war above, and despite the fact that it was the controlling influence on all of our lives, the thrust of these books is about the **social changes** and reactions that took place in this period, here in Oz.

Finally, **let me apologise in advance to anyone I might offend**. In a work such as this, with so many painful memories all round, it is certain some people will think I got some things wrong. I am certain I did, but please remember, all of this is **only my opinion**. And really, **my opinion does not matter one little bit in the scheme of things**. I hope you will say "silly old bugger", and shrug your shoulders and read on.

OUR LEGACY FROM EARLIER YEARS.

At the start of the year, there was no doubt the war was going very well for this nation. In faraway Europe, everywhere you looked, the Germans and their few remaining friends were under the hammer. The British, American and Empire troops were moving in towards Berlin from the west, and were perched virtually on the banks of the Rhine. In the east, Russians had re-taken most of lands over-run earlier by the Germans, and were massing to the east and north of Berlin. As well as these two menacing forces, countries like Greece, Italy, and Hungary were all proving a handful for the Nazis as the partisans there joined with invading Allied troops to chase them away.

In our nearby Pacific and Asia, Australians were helping the Yanks and other Empire forces. **The thought that we in Australia might be invaded had now gone.** Also, as the Americans were now bombing Tokyo and other Japanese cities on a daily basis, and as they re-captured island after island in the Pacific, and as they regained areas in Burma and China, **hopes were growing that maybe the war here would soon be over as well.**

This was a great relief to the people of Australia. For two whole years they had laboured hard, working long hours in the fields and factories to produce materials for a nation at war. As well as that, they had suffered from the introduction of literally thousands of regulations and restraints, as the Government tried to rein in consumption of anything that was not necessary for the war effort. For example, blackouts at night were almost gone now, but rationing of food, clothing linen, butter, sugar and tea were still very much evident.

From a different perspective, all able-bodied men were compelled to join the armed services, mainly the Army. Some however, were excused military service because they worked in a "protected" industry like the coal mines or on the wharves. Everyone else left over was drafted to the Civil Construction Corps (CCC) and sent to anywhere in Oz to do war-related work. Many women also enlisted, some to the women's corps of the armed services, and some to auxiliary services, and some to female versions of the CCC. **Theoretically**, everyone was doing their bit. **In practice** though, there were some who were very artfully dodging any load, but they were a small minority.

At the start of 1945, however, the mood in Oz was changing. While politicians were urging that people should continue on with working long hours for the good of the nation, most of that same nation was saying that **it was fed up with this, given**

that the Japs were now thousands of miles away. Because of this growing attitude, **strikes were popping up all over the place.** Miners, wharfies, butchers, train drivers, tram drivers, factory workers, and heaps of others wanted more pay. They also realised that many of them had accepted conditions of work during the war that were much to the benefit of the bosses. So they wanted better conditions as well as more pay. In any case, **strikes were a constant pain in the neck.**

POLITICS IN OZ

The Labour Party held power in the Federal Parliament, but only by a thread. John Curtin had had the task of leading the nation through the difficult three years of a menacing war, and was well liked and respected by almost everyone. The trouble was that for the last two months, he had been ill, suffering probably from exhaustion, and was completely off the job.

This meant that while the cat was away, the mice were trying to play. In particular, his Deputy, Frank Forde, had just announced that Australia's airlines across the nation would be **nationalised** at an indefinite date, but soon.

Nationalisation was a lively topic at the time. The Labour Party had just held a referendum that sought **to continue all the regulations** into the hopefully-coming period of peace. They wanted this period to last for five years. This meant that they hoped that the austerity, and all the regulations, and all the hard labour that the nation was now suffering, would go on for five years after peace was signed.

Their argument was quite reasonable in a way. In brief, they said that Australia had fought off the enemy because most people had pulled together, and had suffered privation for three years. After the war, and into the future, we could all prosper if the war-time controls were continued on. So, let's have socialism, and as part of that, let's nationalise some industries, like the airlines, and perhaps coal and perhaps the banks.

The opposition, led effectively by Robert Menzies, wanted none of this. They lamented the losses of personal freedom that currently existed, the stifling of free enterprise, and the enormous power that the regulators had to define what could be done and not done. They argued at times that the powers that Labour were seeking were the same as those operating now in Germany and Italy. Surely, they said, we don't want to go down that path.

In any case, the referendum was beaten by a convincing majority. Enter deputy Frank Forde, while Curtin was away. Out came the proposal to nationalise the airlines. We will hear more about this as the year progresses.

MORE ABOUT THE REGULATIONS

By the end of 1944, some regulations had been relaxed. These were, however, a drop in the bucket. Most of the thousands of regulations were still in place. For example, rules on crossing State boundaries and restraints on travelling on interstate trains were still there. The entire Oz world was bound by one regulation after another.

HOW WERE ORDINARY FAMILIES COPING?

Almost every family had at least one member absent from home. They might have been serving anywhere in the Pacific in the armed services, or as civilians in the CCC building aerodromes in the Northern Territory say, or as female factory workers in the munitions factory at Lithgow. Some families had three or four sons away overseas, and probably had no real idea of what was happening to them.

For those families with men in the Forces, life was lived on a knife-edge. Every day the mail-man came and hopefully went on without stopping. When he did stop, the walk to the mailbox was an agony. Would there be a dreaded letter from the Army saying that their son or husband was dead, missing, or wounded? Now, early in 1945, the casualties were diminishing, but when that letter did come, the devastation was still the same. For those who lost menfolk, they might eventually come to cope well enough, but it was coping and nothing more. Their lives were never the same again.

The rest of the population were tired, genuinely tired. **On the one hand**, most of them had worked long hours, for about three years. Many had worked a six-day week and some of them seven days a week. On top of that, in 1943, and 1944, no one was allowed to take a break at Christmas, nor take their annual leave; public holidays were cut to Christmas Day and Good Friday; and recreation such as horse racing was reduced to a few meetings per year.

On the other hand, everyone had been tormented, day and night, by the thought that the Japs would land on our shores and pillage our nation. The possibility of this was emphasised constantly by Government propaganda, by poster and radio and news-reels, that produced graphic stories and cartoons telling of the atrocities in store if the dreaded **yellow peril** invaded. By the end of 1944, only the most pessimistic were worried about this, but it had taken its toll over earlier years, and even now any mention of a military set-back raised the blood pressure of the nation.

One side-effect of the nation being plunged into industry and long working hours was that **people had more money than they had ever had before.** Even though taxation was raised to pay for the war, take-home pay was plentiful. The problem was that it was hard to spend it. **There was nothing to buy.** Real estate sales were prohibited, you needed permission from Canberra to trade in cars, and getting this was well nigh impossible. Clothing and food were rationed, the sale of luxury goods of all types was prohibited, holidays had been forbidden, and most sporting fixtures were cancelled. For example, there was no Test cricket, and no national football competitions of any code. There were no horse races to bet on.

Fortunately, there was one avenue for spending that clever people opened up. It was called the **black market**. Activity here was strictly illegal, and the Government even set up special Courts round the nation to prosecute offenders. But it was very popular among a large section of the community. If you wanted bottles of beer or spirits, or a second-hand car, or a wedding dress, or more sugar for making jam, then you could get it all "on the black". Mind you, you had to pay quite a price for the privilege, but enthusiasts could say that you had to spend your money some way. Where the goods came from, no one ever really figured out, though it was clear that the petrol supplies, and food items such as tinned peaches, came from the military bases.

DEEPLY ENTRENCHED VALUES

Loyalty to Britain. The population here wholeheartedly endorsed the idea that we should give to England any aid we could. This deep-seated loyalty had never wavered, even at the time a few years ago when our troops had been sent pointlessly by Churchill to be slaughtered in Greece and Crete. The Mother Country still had to be defended, and supported with food, and our airmen were still there fighting the Jerries night and day. There was no talk of a republic, the King and Royal family were symbols of all that was British and good, and we still chose our Governors General from the British aristocracy. *God Save the*

King was the national anthem, and we stood, and sometimes saluted, when this anthem was played at the start of the Saturday picture shows.

The White Australia Policy (WAP) was also widely accepted without scrutiny. Even though hundreds of millions of our neighbours to our north had different coloured skin, and spoke different languages, we automatically thought of Australia as a white, British nation that would maintain its superiority by excluding the hordes of lesser folk to the north. By the same token, the Aborigines were also one of the inferior races, and were accorded few of the blessings of our higher civilisation. **Both attitudes would persevere for a long time.**

PROPAGANDA AND CENSORSHIP

The British set up propaganda departments and censorship agencies well before they declared war on Germany in September, 1939. As their war gradually developed, the free flow of information was restricted, and ultimately **only officially-approved news and views were released to the public.** At the same time, censorship restraints were placed on free speech and the expression of opinions, so that subversive speech was illegal and so too was the flow of information that might be of benefit to the enemy.

In Australia, we adopted this same approach, and when Japan started its Pacific invasions at the end of 1941, the Government was quick to impose far-reaching restrictions and punishments on the Australian public. By the start of 1945, these instruments were still in place, and Government bureaus were anxious to continue their repressive measures into the future.

The idea behind all of this was commendable, but it had many faults in practice. Every household in the nation could tell you of some or other abuse of power that they knew of. Letters between families at home and soldiers away, were opened and read, looking for the flow of some inadvertent **so-called** valuable piece of news. People on buses were arrested when they were overheard telling their neighbor of fleet movements that everyone in Sydney already knew about. News of a bombing disaster in Broome was **released to the public more than a year after the event**. A well-known Labour politician tried to suppress purely political criticism of a mate in the newspapers, **supposedly** because of national security. The abuses were widespread, and smacked of a new, untried, and unqualified bunch of bureaucrats with too much power and not enough common sense.

At the same time, the Government poured out volumes of active propaganda. We were told incessantly that our forces were having great victories all over the place, at almost no cost to us, but very dire for the enemy. Day after day, the message came through that our (US and Oz) air forces had fought with the enemy, and that 40 Japs had been shot down and we lost 5 planes. Such exaggerated stories made people distrustful of the propaganda machine, and once again, the bureaucrats exceeded their mandate.

With the enemy now far away, it was time for these security measures to be revised and then reduced. We will see later in the book just how this worked out.

ANOTHER LOOK AT THE CCC

The Civil Construction Corp, the CCC, was often synonymous with another agency called Man-power. They were important and powerful institutions who, between them, had the necessary role of mobilising every man, and many women, into some job that would aid the war-effort. They built bridges, and roads and airfields and factories, and guns and tanks and planes, and so on, with this manpower.

Again, though, they were equally famous at this time for excesses, and glaring mistakes in action and in judgment. I won't go into detail now, apart from saying that they suffered from bureaucratic malfunctions that will attract our attention in the following pages.

WRITING THIS BOOK – THE PROCESS

This book is the seventh in a series of 35 year-books that I am publishing. These 35 books cover the 27 years from 1939 to 1973. For each year-book, I worked my way, day-by-day, though the *Sydney Morning Herald* (SMH) and the *Age/Argus* from Melbourne, and noted the good stories as I went. At the end, I wrote up the best stories, checking as I went with other newspapers as necessary, and with other sources such as the *Women's Weekly*, and *Hansard*. I also spoke to hundreds of oldies and got their memories. At the end, I had a book.

For *1945*, I collected much information, and could have written six books but, in the final selection of material, I think I have covered most of the major issues that people then were interested in. In some cases, I have dwelt a little on minor frivolous matters, perhaps to the detriment of more sober considerations. Still, in the long run, this makes the book more readable, and hopefully it will convey adequately the spirit of the times.

Each of the books is mainly Sydney based, but **I have been deliberately national in outlook**, so that readers elsewhere will feel comfortable that I am talking about matters that affected them personally. After all, housing shortages and strikes and juvenile delinquency involved **all** Australians, and other issues, such as problems overseas, had no State component in them. Overall, I expect I can make you wonder, remember, rage and giggle equally, **no matter where you hail from.**

So, let's get on with it.

JANUARY NEWS ITEMS

The **Germans launched a last-ditch offensive** against the Allies on the western front. Hitler hoped that he could win a surprise victory in the regions to the north of France, and would then be able to turn the tide everywhere else....

By early January, it was clear that he had run out steam and that **the Battle of the Bulge** had been won by the Allies. This Battle was all over by the 15th, when the Germans on this front **had been beaten back to their home soil.**

Movie star, **Charlie Chaplin**, was admitted to hospital with some of his ankle muscles cut. He will remain there for a few days. Police say that he came home late last night, and could not find his keys, **so he kicked in the glass door.** He was returning home with his wife when the incident happened.

Customs officials will intensify their campaign to ensure that **bottled beer will reach hotels**, and not be sold on the black market. Critics said that even if it reached the pubs, **it was still being sold after hours at exorbitant prices in back parlours.**

Press quote, January 3rd. "**Enemy air activity** has directed bombs against southern England during the 24 hours ended dawn today. Damage and casualties were reported." **No further details were given. The Brits were strong on censorship too.** The bombs were actually new **V2 rockets**, which were unreliable, but still caused widespread damage....

The Brits were perplexed because **they could not locate where the bombs were being launched from**. If they knew, they could destroy the sites by bombing. The bombs were causing a lot of damage, and once **again London was under attack**, and worried and frightened.

Nine hundred **Australian brides** of US Servicemen are waiting for a sea passage **to America**. This number includes fiancées.

There **might** be **less than one egg per week** available for each civilian in three months time, poultry experts have forecast. Most new-laid eggs and millions from cold storage would be **needed for our Servicemen and the American troops**.

HMAS Matafele is presumed lost, and her crew of 37 posted as missing. **A reminder that the Navy was losing men as well** as the better-reported Army and Air Force.

Total casualties for all ranks of the armed forces of **the British Empire were 1,043,000.** This was from the outbreak of war in September, 1939, to last November. **Comment: that is a lot of men, and a lot of suffering for families.**

News item, Jan 22nd. After an illness of almost three months, **the Prime Minister, John Curtin, is back at work today**.

In the **Battle of the Bulge, the Nazis lost 150,000 men, killed or taken prisoner.** In a month. They had families too.

January, 29th. **Our new Governor General** arrived in Sydney today and proceeded to Marulan for afternoon tea. As you might expect for such a grand occasion, the reception was held in the police station. **The Duke and Duchess of Gloucester**, and their two children, will perform their vice-regal duties for the next four years.

BULLDOGGING AND BUCKJUMPING

Buckjumping involved taking a horse and tying a coarse thick rope round its loins, putting a rider on it, then pulling the rope tight so that it hurt, and when the horse reacted in pain and started to buck wildly, counting the seconds before the rider was thrown off. **With bulldogging**, a rider on a horse rode up behind a running steer, and dived off his horse, onto the steer's neck and tried to throw the beast to the ground. Again, the time was taken for comparison with other rider contestants.

Every small and big city had a show, or a rodeo, or both, once a year, and there were always crowds of people who would go to the ring to watch these events. The riders were skilful horsemen, without helmets or any protection, and quite of lot of them were youths and ratbags. Still, the crowds turned up every time, and these were very popular events.

Though not with every one. A small minority had a concern, not for the riders, who were often injured, but for the animals. One small Letter stirred up a lot of correspondence.

Letters, C Shaw. The recent accident at the Showground rodeo, in which a bullock broke its leg and had to be destroyed, well illustrates the cruelty of what are known as "bulldogging" contests. I do not know what the popular feeling is on the matter, but I for one have always felt that these events could, and should, be better omitted from horse and cattle shows. The RSPCA's protest against the event is to be applauded.

Letters, A Palmer. If, as the judges at the Police Boys' Club show assure us, the cruel practices of the rodeo are "part of the ordinary routine of station life," all we can say is "more's the pity." But such practices as a necessity are a very different matter to staging them as a show for thousands of callous, unthinking people, who are out for a thrill, providing their own skins are safe. It seems a great pity that the police, who do such fine work with the city boys, should to some extent nullify the good they do by upholding cruelty to animals in any form.

Letters, M Kartzoff. Some sections of the Press and the RSPCA have made statements deprecating the alleged cruelty to animals at a recent "rodeo" on the Showground.

The use of stockwhips is essential, and will never be replaced by fine sentiments in handling recalcitrant bullocks. So is the nose-ring for bulls. Horses will have to be broken-in and one cannot afford to be gentle in the process. Steers have to be thrown for the purpose of branding and castrating. Cows must be broken-in for milking.

Where is the harm in the fact that fine, healthy bushmen, proud of their craft, should be competing and taking their spills like men? After all, Australia is still largely a pioneer country, which should develop "guts" in its youngsters, to fit them to conquer this continent, rather than a false soft-heartedness fit only for the urban population of the old world.

Letters, Animal-Lover. As a visitor to Australia, I have read with very great interest statements by the chairman and secretary of the RSPCA, in which they allege cruelty at a recent Sydney rodeo. It must surely come as a surprise to many Australians and certainly all fair-minded people present at the Showground that this society, so well known for its good intentions and excellent achievements, should so misdirect its endeavours as to propose taking action to ban rodeos and prosecute sponsors of the recent exhibition.

I have witnessed rodeos in various countries and have no hesitation in saying that the conduct of events at the Showground in its humane treatment of animals was superior to anything I have witnessed elsewhere. The proceedings sponsored by the police were in aid of boys' clubs, and the Royal Society hardly shows itself in a favourable light by prosecuting promoters of such a worthy cause and who conducted a rodeo on lines as humane as possible.

Letters, Chas Hall. I agree with Mr Palmer that if the cruel practices of the rodeo are "part of the ordinary routine of station life," more's the pity. But I can assure your correspondent that such is not the case, and those who make such statements do not know their subject.

I have spent sixty years actively amongst cattle in Queensland, the Northern Territory, and New South Wales, and have never seen bulldogging carried out except on a showground. Quite apart from the cruelty of the practice, the average intelligent city man must think we have a very clumsy, slow, and laborious method of handling our cattle.

Your correspondent, Mr Kartzoff, asserts that steers have to be thrown to be branded and castrated, but let me assure that gentleman that on any properly-managed cattle station the calves are all branded at from three to six months of age without any cruelty or hurt except the actual branding. Horses certainly have to be broken in, and cows, too, for milking, but anyone who uses cruelty in the process does not know his job.

Comment. These events were more-or-less gradually banned round the nation, State by State, but 70 years later they still persist in some outback areas. One correspondent from Darwin wrote to me and said "a good steer gets thrown half a dozen times in his life. Compare that with a bad steer who goes off to slaughter three years earlier." There is logic there. Somewhere.

SOCIALISM WAS NOT COMMUNISM

The Americans had always opposed the concept of Communism since Karl Marx spoke up in the mid-nineteenth century. From about 1917, it became a real threat to their capitalist world when the Russians implemented it in the USSR after their revolution. After that, our American friends did everything they could to frustrate and limit and destroy the Red Menace. They correctly thought that the concept of State control of every facet of national life was contrary to the idea of free enterprise and individual freedom. So these two great powers were at logger-heads from that time, and still were until 1942.

In those 25 years, a different philosophy gained much popularity, particularly in Britain and France. This was called **socialism, and it took an in-between stance**. Within the nation, certain large enterprises, for example, the coal mines and the banks, should be controlled by the nation's government, but individual freedoms should be preserved. So, for example, unlike Communism, it would allow for the individual ownership of property, and for the fruits of labour to go to the individual and not the commune.

There was another important distinction between the two philosophies. **To the Russian Reds, the ideal state would be gained by revolution**. That is, by the rising up of the masses, and the armed seizure of power, over the dead bodies of the capitalists. **The Socialists**, distinctly different, wanted to maintain the existing structures of state, and **effect changes by legislation** and other peaceful means.

To you, the reader, the differences must be obvious even from this **grossly simplified description**. The Communists wanted a totalitarian State, brought about by bloody revolution. The Socialists wanted some State control of some industries, but hopefully little else, introduced by gradual change.

The trouble **for our Labour Party** was that in practice, **the two philosophies and followers were all mixed up**. The Labour Party stood for socialism, pure and simple. Yet many of its members wanted all sorts of variations on that, and some wanted huge variations, so that it was hard to tell them apart from Communists. In particular, the trade unions, an essential part of the Labour Party, were led by Communists, so the end result was that the Labour Party was always open to **the charge that its members were "fellow travellers" of the Communists.**

JOSEPH STALIN AND ADOLF HITLER

Things get muddier. **Hitler had in 1942 made a terrible mistake and attacked Russia**, and Germany was then conducting its war on the eastern front as well as in the west. This turned everything upside down, because now the leading Communist nation was joining **with** the big capitalist nations in a massive war.

All of this was a bit of a shock to every Australian because now we were asked to take the lovely Joe Stalin to our hearts, and forget all the ugly stuff we had been fed about how evil Communism and the Russians were. Such a big reversal did not come easily to most Australians.

So, from the middle of 1942 to the end of 1944, and beyond, all we heard about the Russians was about what wonderful allies they were. Under war-time censorship, no one could criticise an ally, and some of our volunteer groups were even sending woollen mittens to their fighters. Truly, we were brothers in war.

WHAT ABOUT THE STRIKES?

This, however, was to ignore the fact that, within Oz, the die-hard Reds were trying to disrupt the nation, particularly by strikes. Then, in late January, 1945, the *SMH* ran an article that **attacked the Communists for their roles in strikes**, and this led to **a stream of pent-up comments from readers** flooding the Herald.

> **Letters, R Rutledge.** While congratulating you on your exposure of the Communist danger in our midst, I express the hope that this will be followed up by detailed examples of the perfidy of this body. Your article dealt with the position on the coalfields very well, but I have in mind another national service which is essential to the proper

carrying on of the war effort, and which is controlled by the Communist Party, i.e., the loading the discharging of ships in all Australian ports.

We read frequently in the Press that the officials of the Waterside Workers' Union are anxious to co-operate with the government in expediting this work, but the public should know that similar procedure is adopted to waterside work as with the mines. For example, the rate of work for handling general cargo in Sydney has been deliberately cut down to 37 per cent of the normal rate in 1939.

The truth is that if the waterside workers were allowed to work with only ordinary diligence, there would be no shortage of labour on the waterfront, and ships would be dispatched in less than half the time now taken, to the great benefit of the war effort, to say nothing of the alleviation of the position regarding the carriage of civilian goods which cannot at present be carried.

Letters, Labourite. The unions are not the sole objects of the Communist attack: **Branches of the Australian Labour Party are also being infiltrated.** The procedure is for Communists to join individually and unostentatiously throughout the year. When the annual meeting takes place they attend en masse and vote a block "ticket." Due to the apathy of the moderates, who almost invariably are caught off guard, the result is the election of the Red elements to all executive offices. The game is then completely in their hands. They hold the books and are vested with great powers under the rules.

Letters, B O Mealey. I feel that I must write to congratulate you on the excellent article on Communism.   I have repeatedly seen evidence of methods used by Communists in their quest for power, but relatively few people realise what your article showed so clearly, that Communists, while active in so many fields, are nevertheless working to an integrated plan and under foreign directions.

Letters, A Hebblewhite. Communism cannot be brushed aside by merely abusing it. To understand it is a prerequisite to successfully opposing it, as we must do in a comparatively short period of time if we are to escape a period of great potential difficulty, if not disaster. In almost every town and district, with or without the co-operation of Labour leagues, the Communist is working to a carefully prepared plan.

The sum total of all these efforts is added support for the Labour Party, which they virtually control through the unions. Driving force and advanced thinking have firmly established this leadership. Service men and women are joining carefully sponsored organisations in large numbers. Some of them do not realise until they are admitted to membership that the organisation is working for ultimate Sovietisation.

An effective political party organisation opposed to Labour is necessary, but it is not the complete answer. Of itself, it is entirely inadequate, and must be supplemented by an "opposite number" to the Communist organisation, planning and working for the democratic State in a non-party atmosphere. It must originate with the people, and be devoted entirely to their interests as distinct from any section. Any political party representing moderate views gains strength and stature from a live organisation, and unconsciously turns to meet popular demands.

Comment. Is he anti-Communist? Or anti-Labour? He is not too sure. He would say, I suppose, that he is anti-both.

Letters, B M Morrissey. For many years the Communists have had a monopoly on propaganda amongst the workers of this country, and have been able to build up **the greatest political organisation that this country has yet seen** in their endeavour to seize power by revolution and destroy our Australian way of life.

The great majority of workers are opposed to this foreign influence, but by their apathy have allowed themselves to come under its control. Your article will serve to awaken many of them from their dangerous sleep, and to those of us who have been trying to carry on the fight is a source of consolation and inspiration, judging by comments passed at my place of employment. Compulsory voting at union elections held under independent returning officers is the only way to overcome the menace.

Letters, Rupert W Wallace.   May I offer my sincere congratulations upon your full page exposure of the evils of Communism?   It is long since due that the general public should be enlightened as to the true aims of our local branch of revolutionists, and I am glad that a daily paper with the distinguished record of your own should be the one to fire the first shot.

Letters, G Grahme.   When the war is over, and Russia is no longer our ally, I wonder whether we will be more critical of the Communists within us than we are now.

Comment.   In the last of these Letters, Mr Grahme is battling with the censors. What I suspect he really wants to say is that "we have a number of subversives within our ranks who are working to change our society by revolution. We are, however, constrained from facing up to this by our war-time commitment to Russia. Perhaps we will do this after the war."

We will hear a lot more about the Communists and strikes as the year progresses.

YOUNG GIRLS GETTING INTO TROUBLE

Young girls across the nation were entering a strange new world, very different from the world that their mothers were brought up in. The old model of the family had been destroyed in many cases, by the father joining the military or the CCC, and the mother perhaps having a job or volunteer work that took her away for much of the day. That is, parental control and example was nowhere near what it had been in the past. At the same time, all sorts of taboos and restrictions on the young daughters were being questioned, and the Americanisation of young-girl society was proceeding at a rapid rate. This impassioned Letter takes a good look at the developing dangers.

Letters, Catherine Furby. A small army of social workers goes on doing its best to help children to make an adjustment, after they have been before the Children's Court, bitterly conscious of the lack of any real interest in this most urgent social problem. The commonest accepted reason for girls becoming delinquent is that their parents allow them to run wild. It is so easy for those who have no children to dismiss this deplorable social phenomenon in this way. We are told that their mothers are pleasure-mad, and in some cases it is so, but in many more cases the parents have done their feeble best against the forces of outside attraction and their children's own desires, to keep them from temptation, and such parents spend many anxious hours seeking their daughters in the city streets.

In many cases the home environment is one that makes it practically impossible for the child not to become delinquent, but in a large percentage the causes lie elsewhere. By the time that girls reach the stage of defying their parents and staying out late associating with servicemen in most harmful promiscuity, they are generally beyond reclamation. I do not mean to imply that they are forever-after committed to a life of degradation, but that excitement is necessary to them and nothing matters except the satisfaction of the craving for all kinds of excitement.

No amount of reasoning will alter the position. All the girl's experience so far has taught her that to be more attractive than her sisters is to scale the heights of feminine achievement. Thus we have the existing state of affairs where thousands of girls of tender years are parading the city streets, flashily dressed and heavily disguised with brilliant make-up, so that the city is just one vast shop window displaying human wares. Who will dare to say that girls themselves are to blame?

Recently at a small suburban concert I saw a child of about nine years give a turn which for suggestiveness would have done great, if doubtful, honour to the most experienced vaudeville comedienne. A doting mother took her infant by the hand and led her from the stage to the back of the hall through a surge of adulation. This sort of thing is happening in amateur concerts everywhere and might be acceptable to more or less indiscriminating audiences, but what is it doing to the children?

At an open-air vaudeville show last week, the first three rows were almost exclusively of children aged from about five to 14 years. The crude filthiness of most of the jokes did not shock me. It did not shock the children either. They shrieked with laughter. However, as a Children's Court probation officer, I was profoundly shocked that such things should be allowed to happen.

To eliminate all unhealthy stimulants to the natural instincts of children, and to guard them from unwholesome excitement in public entertainment, would do a great deal to lessen child delinquency. The ruination of young girls does not begin at teen age. It begins when they first become exposed to the ceaseless blinding light of eroticism which beats upon them in picture-show matinees and similar entertainment – that is, at about the age of three.

ONE VIEW OF HOUSIE-HOUSIE

Letters, A F Brown. The "Herald" recently it was said that "housie-housie is one of the most popular games at charity and Church carnivals." The statement appears to be misleading as it seems to involve all the Churches. As a member of the Presbyterian Church I can definitely state that gambling of any kind (including housie-housie) for the raising of funds is not permitted by this Church.

FEBRUARY NEWS ITEMS

Coloured pipes for women are becoming popular in USA. They have daintier bowls, graceful stems, and coloured plastic mouthpieces, which are inter-changeable to match an ensemble. In the past three months, 200,000 have sold. Coloured tobacco pouches are being made to match the pipes.

Sargent's Limited has announced that it will **increase the price it charges for its pies.** Previously costing three pence, the pies will now cost three and a half pence. **In its many cafes**, the price for a pie, cup of tea, and a roll will be 16 pence. **These rises have been approved after a successful application to the Prices Commission.**

The War Cabinet has decided that **all air-raid shelters** in the nation may now be **dismantled.** Northern Territory is the only exception.

The People's Court of Sophia, according to Moscow Radio, has **sentenced to death**, on charges of treason, three **Members of the Bulgarian Council of Regency**. There were 100 other persons also sentenced to death. This marked **the beginning of the killing of those persons, in all European countries, who had collaborated with Germans.** The **kangaroo courts** pretended to be guided by justice, but were really instruments of revenge....

At their execution, 50,000 people demonstrated in the streets shouting **"Death to Fascists"** and **"death to the murderers of our people."**

Beginning next month, **10,000 surplus Army motor cycles will be released** to the public this year.

Huge Paddy's **Markets** will be set up in each State to dispose of Army **second-hand materials.**

A reminder that **strikes were a daily feature of life at the moment.** News item: "Sydney's meat supplies and important ship repair work are threatened by strikes. Homebush abattoirs may close today." Just a typical day.

News item, February 10th. **A special train** left Sydney tonight taking **330 Land Army girls to South Australia** to harvest the crop of dried fruits for the Services.

The Royal Navy is rationing leave in Sydney because of a shortage of beds. Most of the sailors have been on board for months, and are **somewhat anxious** to leave the ship.

News item. February 20th . The Allies are **invading Iwo Jima**, 740 miles from Tokyo. **There are 800 ships involved in the attack. Comment:** a massive force. The Iwo Islands are the first bit of **Japanese** territory to fall to the Allies.

800,000 butter coupons have been stolen from the office of the Rationing Commission.

Canberra will spend 175,000 Pounds on a plant for the mass production of the **new wonder drug penicillin.**

A **"canvas hotel"** with **beds for sailors** has been erected in Sydney's Hyde Park. This will provide beds and snacks of pies, tea and fruit. **The marquee and other provisions were erected in 24 hours.** 150 indoor beds were also made available at the Showground, and 200 in Manly.

Four hundred thousand people in Melbourne welcomed the **Duke and Duchess of Gloucester** in a street parade yesterday. Royalty is popular in Oz.

THE WAR IN EUROPE

In January, and all through February, the Allied forces had success after success. **On land**, no matter where you looked, on the eastern front **or** the western front **or** in Italy **or** in the Balkans and beyond, their armies won victories and marched ever-onwards toward Berlin. **In the air**, thousands of bombers, protected by fighters, attacked day and night, and devastated cities and towns. Citizens were in no way spared, and their homes, here today, were gone a few minutes later. The destruction of bridges and dams and factories and railways was inevitable and rampant. The slaughter was beyond belief, and **both sides were suffering**. **No one was winning this war.**

Hitler was having a hard time. His health was poor, and he was always hoping that somehow his forces would have a few victories that would turn the tide. Some of his generals thought that the situation was hopeless, and that he should sue for peace. **Hitler would have none of that traitorous talk**, and commanded his forces to fight to the last bullet in every battle. The noose was rapidly tightening, but a loyal citizenry, and most of the army, were not going to accept that the situation was beyond recall as yet.

In the dozen or so liberated nations, now once again free to govern themselves, the removal of the Nazis did not bring peace and contentment. Apart from the immense tasks of reconstruction, and **the immediate problem of starvation**, there were political problems. **On the eastern front**, the Russians were claiming that **they** should set up controls and establish boundaries that were not welcome in the home state.

In other nations, for example Poland, there were conflicts between two major groups. **On the one hand**, there was the so-called provisional government that had fled to England before the Nazis arrived. **On the other**, there were groups that had stayed and resisted the German-led forces, and helped in the liberation. Who should govern? Then there were the Russian occupiers. They wanted boundaries fixed **here**, and the disorganised Poles wanted them **there**, and the Brits wanted them **somewhere else**. Such disputes led to many armed clashes.

In Greece, the situation erupted into civil war. As the Germans were driven out, **two** partisan armies helped the Brits. At the end of hostilities, **both camps wanted control,** and actual civil war broke out for a few months. The Brits stepped in, and restored order. But such conflicts sowed the seeds for ongoing armed actions in the future.

For all of these nations, no matter what particular problems they faced, the goal of real peace was still a long way off.

THE WAR IN ASIA AND THE PACIFIC

The war against Japan was going just as well. At the end of February, General MacArthur was now in the position where he could brag, **as only he could**, about returning to the Philippines. The Americans were in the process of cleaning up Iwo Jima, and the Australians were doing the dirty work of smoking out the left-behind Japs from north New Guinea and the Solomons.

By now, Tokyo and other Japanese cities were within range of American bombers, so daily air-raids were mounted and were causing fearful destruction and fire-storms. The Japanese fleet was holed up at various locations, and though still substantial, was not prepared to risk going to sea because of its fear of annihilation. In all, the odds were that our successes would be continued, and that if the Germans conceded in say two months, then the Japs might do likewise in five.

At least, this is what the optimists in Oz thought. For many, though, this was too good to be true, and there was the nagging worry that somehow the Japs would stage a comeback. We will wait and see if they did.

PREFERENCE FOR SERVICEMEN

When our menfolk were going off to war, promises were made to them that, after the war, they would come home to their old jobs, and that they would get preference in the allocation of houses to live in. So, now, with peace maybe just round the corner, the nation's top bodies were working out how this might be achieved in practice.

In particular, the Federal Cabinet was setting some rules that would apply. They said that if a returned serviceman applied for a job after the war, and also a non service-man applied, then if all other things were equal, the job would go to the former. The same would apply to rental housing.

They added that soldiers who served **overseas** would go to the top of the list, and those who **served longer** would also be well placed. One provision that was controversial was that it was up to the **employer** to sort out just who he employed, and if there was an objection, then it could be referred to an appeals tribunal. This allowed a great deal of freedom for the employer to manipulate if he so choose, and indeed it was a freedom greatly used in the future.

Still, the rules as set out seemed reasonable enough, but there were some who objected. In particular, trade unions wanted **similar protections for union members** over non-members. This was a hurdle for the union-dominated Labour Party, and it was at the moment rattling round trying to satisfy both sets of preferences. For example, it was suggesting that service preference would apply for seven years, and after that union preference would take over.

Some people had interesting attitudes to the proposed law.

Letters, F A Keen. They say it is not fair to give preference to the men who fought because some munition workers wanted to enlist and were prevented. With due respect to such munition workers, the fact is, that they did not enlist, and the fighting soldier did.

The Utopian cry is raised "Work for All," therefore preference will be unnecessary. What a reed for the returning soldier to rest his hopes upon! An object well worthy of striving for, but a dream yet to be converted into reality. The same specious plea was raised when we could have got immigrants but would not have them until "not a man was unemployed." Whilst awaiting the dawn of the glorious day heralding "jobs for all," there rests upon us an obligation, the honouring and redemption of a pledge implied and implicit, made to the men who went forth to battle for the salvation of Australia.

Letters, George Vincent. Any scheme of preference which merely aims at ensuring that a returned soldier obtains and retains a job will be doomed to failure. Before a returned soldier applies for a position it must be certain that he is as capable of occupying that position as those who did not see service. Anything less would be unfair to industry. If the returned soldier does not measure up to that standard, then, as a minimum, he must be trained and educated to a state of equality with his more fortunate brother.

Letters, F A Keen. Soldiers, sailors, and airmen when enlisting did not, as a condition for such enlistment, ask for preference. It was a voluntary and spontaneous promise made by the leader of the nation, and accepted by all whose safety then was in imminent jeopardy. To me, therefore, the question is a simple cardinal one affecting the morals of the nation as to whether a pledge made by the leader of the nation is to be honoured by the nation.

I wonder why so many objections and suggestions wrapped in clever verbiage were not made in the dark days, and only when war clouds are drifting from our shores.

Letters, M C Critchley. I was very much astonished by Mr O Schreiber's reactionary attitude regarding the position of women, both now and in the post-war world. I thought all fair-minded thinking people realised that the past and present problem of cheap female labour, with its unsatisfactory results, can only be solved by breaking down all discriminations against women workers.

One basic wage for both men and women would do away with exploitation of female labour, returned men would not be kept out of their jobs, and women wage-earners would not feel the injustice of having their work underpaid. As for the "unfairness of women's competition with men for men's jobs," this applies equally to men's competition with men. What about the many widows and single women with dependents? Have they not as much or more right to jobs than single men with no dependents?

All women cannot "retire and settle down to home life," as Mr Schreiber says they should. If women are capable and skilful, is it fair they should be kept back from specialising in industry? It is an insult to talk about "women's inroad in these directions." In some industries it has been proved that women are more deft and skilful than men. It is time we left off talking about men's jobs and women's jobs, and let both men and women do the work that they are best fitted for, whether it be working in industry, in the professions, or looking after a home and children.

Letters, Paul Mason. I would remind Mabel Critchley that the typical man has a family to support, while a single woman has only her cosmetics habit to support. Typically, she pays only a token sum to board with her parents.

Until the structure of our society changes, the married man with children should earn a lot more that single women.

Letters, Bruce Jenkins. It is wrong to give job preference to anyone. Many of our servicemen fought bravely for our country, but that does not mean that they are qualified to do a certain job. Giving preference will mean thousands of people doing work that they have no aptitude for, and there will be no way of shifting them.

Letter, Council Officer, Sydney. I am an employment officer working for a public authority. I expect that soon I will have to choose between a returned serviceman just back from the war, and the man who has done a particular job very well for three years. Neither man will have any certificates to prove their competence, only their service records.

I will have to employ the ex-serviceman, and sack the other man. I know that he can do the job perfectly, and the odds are that the ex-serviceman will not. So a perfectly good man goes, and the other perhapser takes his place.

I can assure you that when I place advertisements for a job, I will always do it so that **satisfactory incumbents will always be the only ones who can satisfy the requirements.**

Comment. The policy of preference for ex-servicemen was passed into law in the fields of employment and housing. It served its purpose well, for decades, and despite the many abuses, and the many disputes, did help the returned men settle back in.

HOUSING

Soon after the war in the Pacific started, the Federal Government brought down laws that stopped the building industry in its tracks. For house construction, it forbade the construction of new dwellings, and made it almost impossible to renovate the old ones. For landlords, **it froze rents for at least the duration**

of the war. While this was good for tenants, it removed any incentive for landlords to build, or renovate, even if they were allowed to. So a housing shortage quickly developed, and it got worse every year. It took many forms.

Letters, A Soldier's Wife. My husband recently came down on leave, and with him I **walked** everywhere to try to rent a cheap room. We met with no success. All we could get was at One Pound a day, which sum did not include our meals. Incidentally, my allowance is 5 Pounds 12 shillings a fortnight, which I had to use. Is this the sort of thing my husband and the rest of our boys are fighting for and offering their lives?

Letters, A G Huie. Many are willing and anxious to build, have land, and their own labour. They may also have some materials. All they need is some additional materials, and houses will be built – subject to council supervision. Adjoining water mains, there are about 80,000 vacant areas. That is the land that should be built on instead of going out further.

Comment. When the CCC drafted people to country areas, the locals had no way of providing housing. So the government sometimes placed pre-fabricated houses on convenient areas, and leased them to tenants until they were moved on to somewhere else. For example, a large so-called shanty town was built near Griffith for the housing of seasonal fruit pickers. Other towns had more permanent residents.

Letters, C O Wilkinson. As a resident of one of the so-called "shanty" towns for a period of 12 months, I wish to counter in some measure the erroneous picture your staff reporter has drawn of the conditions. The buildings are erected on blocks of ground measuring 48 feet by 90 feet, which is more than many houses that are not "shanties" can boast. The houses are two and three bedroom types. They have built-in shelves and cupboards, a fuel stove, a fuel heater, fuel bath-heater, and fuel copper. The laundry is built on one end of the back verandah. They are very comfortable and convenient inside, the outside appearance being their worst feature.

The tenants are drawn from varied walks of life to start war industries. As for the houses being dirty, the percentage of dirty ones would be no higher than in any other community. In fact it would probably be smaller, as the places, being small and new, are more easily kept clean. The fact of the houses being built of fibro-cement should not condemn them in any way, as it is a well-proven material and is used in buildings of every description.

In view of the scandalous shortage of housing it is nothing short of criminal to decide to pull these places down immediately the war ends. It is far wiser to think of building better places first.

Comment. The restriction on raising rents persisted until the 1960's, by which time landlords had pulled all their hair out. The other restrictions on house **building** were slowly lifted, and the governments kicked in by building Housing Commission houses and **balloting** these out mainly to lucky ex-servicemen. But right through till 1970, housing remained in short supply, and restrictions on the type of house you could build were severe, particularly at the local Council level.

LAMENTS

Throughout the war, most people accepted the hard work, and the austerity, as a necessary evil to save Australia. Also, there was no suggestion that rationing should be reduced or removed, because of the knowledge that it was helping our Motherland, Britain, to survive.

Such thoughts however did not stop people from grizzling. It seemed that every person had a different grouch every day, and gained a great deal of pleasure in talking about it. This is not to say that such complaints were not justified. Many of them, in fact, most of them, were the consequences of poor oversight of the many rules and regulations that the government had imposed. But complaining had become a national pastime, and moaning had reached Olympian proportions. I publish some laments below so you can be up-to-date with what people were bitching about at the time.

Letters, G Kater. On Saturday, January 27, I happened to be present with my children when the ABC children's hour commenced at 5.30pm. Part of the programme consisted of a so-called "Brain's Trust." A very debatable subject was brought forward, namely, "The Right of Inheritance," and to my amazement only one aspect of the subject was put forward. A province in Canada was mentioned, which had imposed, as an experiment, death duties of 50 per cent, but - so stated the programme - this did not go far enough.

The programme then went on to paint a post-war Elderado, including long, fully-paid holidays for everyone, free medical attention, and free medicines. The argument appeared to be that, by imposing 100 per cent death duties, this state of affairs would automatically be achieved. The whole trend was curiously reminiscent of a pamphlet I have just received, published by the Katoomba branch of the Australian Communist Party.

It seems very ominous that such propaganda should now be included in broadcasts to children.

Letters, R F Poate, Picton. This district has suffered seriously. As a result of the "grow more potatoes campaign," when farmers were appealed to by the Government to increase their areas under this crop in order to achieve a certain goal, growers of this district who contracted to grow potatoes last spring are thousands of pounds out of pocket.

Although my own losses are not as great as those of some, my bitter experience would be typical and can be taken as an example. Twelve acres were planted, at a **cost of 141 Pounds**, growing and harvesting costs amounted to 40 Pounds. The cheque received for potatoes marketed amounted to 16 Pounds, from which, commission and other charges amounting to 3 Pounds, and freight to Sydney of 2 Pounds, were deducted, **leaving a balance of 9 Pounds**.

How is the grower to recover from these recurring losses when there are fixed ceiling prices operating on whatever he manages to grow and misunderstanding officials to listen to his complaints and protests?

Letters, Traveller. While circumstances may prevent for the present the reintroduction of sleepers and additional train service for long-distance travellers, will the authorities explain why electric fans installed in first- class carriages have been removed at a time when they are most needed? Their removal, with temperatures soaring around the 100-110 mark, appears to be entirely unwarranted.

Letters, Returned RAAF. I have just returned from active service with the RAAF in England, where I saw 17-year-old girls driving fire engines under battle conditions, and I was shocked to read of our local firemen's strike. Those girls did not strike when they had to drive to fires with German bombs falling about them. The firemen did not strike when they worked for weeks: on duty seven days a week, 24 hours a day, to save London and its heroic people.

When will Australia realise that such stories of our home front war effort make people abroad wonder what we are fighting for?

Letters, Mother of Five. One hears and reads much lately about the shortage of women for the fruit picking and canning. It is beyond my understanding why widows drawing pensions who are struggling to carry on have not been allowed to undertake this work without losing their pensions. I know some who are willing and anxious to work – and are sorely in need of the pay offered.

MARCH NEWS ITEMS

Three deaths from **infantile paralysis (polio)** were reported in Oz last month.

Mr Coles was an Independent member of the Australian Senate. He was **the founder of the Coles stores** that still trade in many parts of Australia. He said recently in Parliament that "you can **buy on the black-markets of capital cities anything you want** that is controlled or rationed, if you are willing to pay the price, and take the risk of being associated with crooks and gangsters"....

He went on to say that **the leniency of the Courts** had largely contributed to the growth of the black-marketing evil. Certain judges seemed to have a different view from that of the Government.

The Japanese, because of their treatment of internees in Manila, **have lost any right to further consideration as a civilised nation**. So wrote Jack Percival, the *SMH* war correspondent. Percival had been interned by the Japs for 37 months, and was recently released.

A boy was accidentally shot dead in the Sydney suburb of Bankstown when he **was playing with a revolver in a sentry box**.

Starvation is rife in Holland because the fleeing **Germans opened up dams to slow down the Allies. There are few pumps for** drainage, so that water is lying in the low lands for months.

More that **2,000 people** have been invited to a **civil reception for the Duke and Duchess of Gloucester** at the Sydney Town Hall next week. **Were you one of the lucky ones?**

Do you still go out onto the street at night and **play marbles under the street light?**

About **200 Australian civilians**, who have been waiting for a **passage home from New Zealand**, will land in Sydney today, after waiting **for up to six months for a berth.**

Well-known French actor and entertainer **Maurice Chevalier** has been **refused a permit to enter England.** He had been engaged to do a 10-week tour, but access was refused on the grounds that **his visit would make no contribution to the war effort.** Earlier, he had been suspected of collaborating with the Germans, but he was cleared of that charge.

News item. March 12. The Society of **British Aircraft Constructors** reveals that the British Government has ordered **a jet-propelled airliner.** So far, it claims, **no other country has embarked on a similar project.**

In Eire, the County of Monaghan has re-affirmed its ruling that **males and females must separate** when they go to the local cinema. **Males must sit on one side, and females on the other**, unless they are married.

Dates will be on sale in Sydney grocery stores soon.

Sydney's Home Mission Society was planning to create a new centre for **delinquent girls.** It would be on a scale, **"never before attempted in the world".** It will teach the girls **nursing, dress-making, cooking, crafts-work, music, folk-dancing, and interior decorating.**

In Britain, **the Archbishop of York** said, in the House of Lords, that **Nazi German arch criminals should be executed without trial.** Dr Garbett said this applied to "Hitler, Himmler and his gang." **Do you agree?**

MILITARY CONSIDERATIONS

While the Americans were conquering the glamorous targets of Philippines and Iowa Jima, the Australians were hived off to the lesser job of **mopping up behind the American forces.** This was a particularly dirty job. The Japs had been isolated on the shores of northern New Guinea, and Bougainville, and dozens and dozens of South Pacific islands, for a couple of years. They were forgotten by the war and basically left to rot. In that period, they had built vast sets of booby-trapped tunnels and catacombs that were almost impregnable to heavy bombardment, and could only be captured by close-range fighting, often hand-to-hand.

The Australians were given the task of clearing out these ferocious warriors. This carried no glamour, no flag-waving triumphant victories, no American bally-hoo that MacArthur excelled in. All that the Aussie soldier could expect after destroying one Jap dug-out was the prospect of another one.

Many of our young and adventurous soldiers were resentful of this because the Yanks were getting all the glory, but taking no more of a risk. Our young daredevils wanted more of the action, and indeed a number of them smuggled themselves onto military planes, and flew to US bases, with the hope of joining the American forces. Most often they failed, and returned to our own Army to face a court martial. But their actions drew attention to the fact that Oz forces were simply dragging the Japs out of their foxholes, and killing them. They saw no military necessity to do that, given that these poor unfortunates had long been abandoned by their own Forces.

As well as that, there was a question, expressed by no less a person than Robert Menzies, as to whether all our efforts to get the Japs out of their dugouts, had been necessary at all. We could equally as well, went the Menzies argument, have simply left them there on their remote islands. This was an argument that continues to be discussed to this day.

WAS OUR ARMY EQUIPPED PROPERLY?

This question was raised by two Letters to the *SMH*.

Letters, Backache, Sydney. The picture of Australian troops toiling up a mountain side with heavy loads of water was an illustration of the lack of modern equipment which is handicapping our men. Despite many complaints from men on the spot, Senator Fraser claims that their equipment "in basic weapons" was second to none. Picks, shovels, and cans of water are, I presume, basic weapons. I, like many other Servicemen, have seen the Americans provide running tap water within a few days of capturing a new sector. They certainly would not carry water on their backs when a pipeline and pump could be used.

Letters, Ex-Capt, AIF. At this late stage in the war it is surprising to read that "doubt" still exists in the minds of those in authority that the American fighting man is better equipped than the Australian. Every Australian soldier knows that this is, of course, the truth. Practically every item of equipment issued to his American counterpart excels that issued to the Australian in weight, fire-power, and up-to-dateness.

While not quarrelling with simple manufacturers' quality, it is a truism to say that the Australian is still equipped with old-fashioned and clumsy equipment. Quite apart from the vast quantities of mechanical equipment for every conceivable purpose used by the Americans, while picks and shovels are the chief engineering tools for Australian troops, I would like to quote a few comparisons in personal equipment.

The most important is, of course, the basic weapon, the rifle. The Americans have the up-to-date automatic Garand rifle on general issue to all ranks. The Australian Lee Enfield bolt-action is a poor weapon in comparison.

The rifle we give our men is practically the same model we used in the Boer War.

Other items of equipment, such as the heavy, overlong, clumsy bayonet, heavy webbing equipment, steel helmet of 1939 design (the Germans and Americans have had splendid helmets for many years), water-bottle weighing three times as much as the American "canteen" bottle, pack and haversack of extremely limited capacity – all these have long been improved upon and replaced by the American Army.

Finally, a sore point with our men in the tropics is the fact that every American is equipped with a good canvas stretcher, but nothing like this is supplied to Australians, in spite of the fact that every man is warned on landing in the tropics that, unless it is absolutely unavoidable, he must not sleep on the ground. Many hundreds of our men have died from scrub typhus contracted in this way.

The Yanks had better and more tanks, more aircraft, better big guns and flame throwers and ducks, planes, aircraft carriers, tractors, and anything you like to mention. The Yanks could land on an island, and within an hour, start making tracks, or airfields, or even **digging out** Japs from their dugouts. For this they had their tractors, rollers and the like. Australian forces had little of this. So, the fact that we were left to do the dirty work of cleaning up behind the Yanks partly reflected the reality that we were not equipped to do the invasive work.

WHY WERE WE SO POORLY EQUIPPED?

In March, criticism was levelled at the Australian Government and Curtin because our Army was not properly equipped. After a lot of mindless discussion, it turned out that it was clear that the Army had adequate supplies of only "basic" materials such as guns and ammunition. As for the other equipment, we simply were not a big, innovative industrial nation, inventing and manufacturing our new products and then mass producing them.

This was a reality, a fact of life. America **was** such a nation, and could send her troops into battles with limited risk to her troops. We, still a minnow, could not.

Of course, the explanation was clouded by politics. As the analysis developed, it appeared that it was a shortage of shipping that was now the cause. That in turn, brought criticism of the wharf-labourers who were infamous for their slow rate of working, and for their multitudinous strikes. This then brought criticism of the Government because of its reluctance to push the wharfies for greater production. So, it was a great political mess. What came out of it was the realisation that our Forces were now making just a little contribution to actively winning the war, and this would doubtless reduce our status at any subsequent peace talks.

WHY WORRY ABOUT IT?

It was clear that after the war, the Big Three nations would make all the decisions about what form the peace would take. It was also clear that the smaller nations, who had played an important part in the war, would be thrown some crumbs. So for Australia, it was now important that its role in the war should be seen as of greater rather than of less significance.

Where did we stand in the glory hunt? As it turned out, we were not well placed at all. The American Press, and large numbers of journalists and many politicians in America, were doing their best to **boost the US national ego** by saying that the **Americans were winning all wars single-handedly**, and that the other Allies were not doing their bit. This **mischievous and utterly false opinion** was getting a lot of mileage among the US population and, in Australia's case, was causing great concern to our leaders. Thus, the Americans got all the newspaper glory, and Australians were getting very little.

So much so, that many Americans were publicly broadcasting the view that we in Australia were not pulling our weight. Not surprisingly, our political leaders were distressed by such idiotic claims, and extracted some promises from the various US authorities that these views would be countered. Of course, this was not possible, and so the non-stop adulation of America's efforts to the detriment of everyone else continued.

Comment. All of these considerations were remarkable at the time because they **were made public**. Even six months earlier, **any suggestion that our forces were being killed for a dubious military advantage would never have made the Press**. Likewise, any suggestions that the post-war division of spoils might depend on international political machinations, **rather than perfect justice**, would have also stayed in the censor's clipping room.

CLERGY IN THE NEWS

Early in the war years, many people had turned to the churches and to prayer for consolation and comfort. The numbers attending church services increased, and their messages from the pulpit were given good prominence in the Press.

Over the last year or so, the sense of urgency had been removed from most people, and so **the public role of the churches** was decreased. Last year, the only time they grabbed the public's attention was when they were roundly criticised for keeping to their set sermons from the pre-war years, and it was claimed they did not have enough to say on the enormous forces of evil that had beset the world since. It was said people wanted **social** commentary, in this bitter world where hatreds and wars surrounded them. To draw lessons from the Bible was stretching the point too far, and they found that the Christian preachings, such as those of forgiveness, were too hard to stomach in the face of torture and mutilation of our POWs by Japanese forces.

So it was appropriate now that a clergyman stuck his head over the parapet and voiced some strong opinions.

News item. The greatly increasing number of divorces posed the question whether divorces would soon equal marriages, the Bishop of Armidale, Dr J S Moyes, said at the inaugural meeting of the New South Wales Branch of the Alliance of Honour last night. "The time of a separate morality for the sexes has passed," Dr Moyes said. "Women have adopted the same standards as the men during the past few years. The standards are lower".

> In the past men were expected to give way to temptation, but not the women. Nowadays, there are good-time girls on many street corners just waiting to be picked up. Dress was never meant to hide shame, but to cover holiness. Nowadays, it is exploited wantonly to tempt people.
>
> Never have we been more in need of some constructive way of teaching the community to understand the true relationship of men and women.
>
> People must be taught that the making of a home is the hardest thing anyone was ever asked to do – it is far beyond romance.
>
> The business world has been guilty of jeopardising the happiness of many marriages by condemning boys and girls to wait until they are 36 or 39 before they are wed.
>
> In the earlier, passionate years, the young couples should be laying the foundations for their families.

Criticising general disunity in the community, Dr Moyes said: "Society has adopted divorce as its theme, there is divorce between employer and employee. There is an entire lack of understanding between town and country and division between men and the land."

The Alliance of Honour is a Protestant inter-denominational missionary organisation, "formed to fight for the principles of purity and decency and to foster the ideal of Christian men and women."

Comment. There were few clergymen who would have disagreed with his main thesis. **Divorce was still uncommon in Australia**, though the war was having the effect of increasing its incidence. Since then, as the years have rolled on, the incidence of divorce has steadily increased. But in 1945, the Bishop spoke for most of the population, and subsequent Letter-writers applauded him.

GOING BACK TO NEW GUINEA

Before the Japs invaded New Guinea in 1942, they bombed all the large settlements in the Australian territory. Port Moresby naturally attracted most of this attention.

The white citizens there, and in the plantations, were quickly evacuated under emergency conditions. This meant that in most cases they were given only a few days to pack whatever they could carry, and be ready for allocation to whatever transport could be found for them.

They were shipped to the Australian mainland, mainly Darwin, leaving behind their houses, their goods, their plantations and memories. It was a time of great drama, and sorrow, and anxiety. As they left the Territory, their houses and properties were ransacked, sad to say, mainly by the troops who remained behind.

In 1945, the Territory was still under military rule, and most of the evacuees were still forbidden permission to re-enter. They had by now formed various pressure groups with the aim of gaining compensation for their ransacked or destroyed property, and for the purpose of regaining entry.

No one in Canberra would tell these poor unfortunates anything about their future, and these Letters below are a soulful plea for some information, and some action, on the matter.

Letters, E James, Pacific Territories Association. The Pacific Territories Association representing the European residents of the Territories of Papua and New Guinea, wishes to record its appreciation of your leading article "Papua and New Guinea," of last Thursday, and to express the keenest disappointment at the Government's continued disregard of the rights and interests of European residents of the Territories. After three years, they still ask in vain when they will be permitted to return to their homes and businesses, although it is admitted by everyone that there is no reason why there should not be a resumption of civil occupation.

It appears that, after three years, the Commonwealth Government is still without a plan for the administration and reoccupation of these territories, and still has to decide questions of policy. About two years ago this Association asked the Government to set up an advisory committee, including representatives of all interests, to assist in this planning. The request was ignored. Nearly 12 months ago, residents petitioned the Government to consider their interests in any plans formulated, and begged that residents might be consulted before their future administration was decided upon. This also was ignored.

Now, to their further dismay, they learn of a decision to govern the country by means of National Security Regulations of complete bureaucratic control – even as to which particular resident may be allowed to return – a total abolition of all citizen rights, and the utmost vagueness as to when, if at all, they may return home. The continued uncertainty and the impossibility of making plans for rehabilitation are imposing unnecessary hardship on those who already have suffered considerably by enforced evacuation.

We ask only for replies to a few simple questions – and by this time, surely, the government should be able to answer them without further procrastination. Is it intended to restore "normal" administration and private enterprise in the territories? If so, when? Does the Government believe European residents have a right to any voice in the administration of the territories in which they reside? If so, by what means is this right to be exercised? Will the Government give as assurance, if normal civil activities are to be restored, that all former residents will be given equal opportunity for return to their homes and for rehabilitation?

If the answer to any of these questions is a negative, we suggest that answer be given at once, when residents can decide how best to make a fresh start in some place outside these unfortunate territories.

Letters, A D F R,. How typical is the official name of the proposed provisional civil administration for New Guinea – "The Provisional Administrative Service for Papua and Liberated Areas under Australian Administration in New Guinea!" I have tried to get some short term by use of initials, but can only suggest "Pang."

Surely this set-up is the bureaucrats' dream of heaven, from the name itself to the absolute disregard of everyone's rights. The whole government of this vast territory will be in the hands of the Canberra clerks, who can make, break, and ignore laws merely by writing a regulation and having it gazetted under the National Security Act.

All this is being done without consulting the European residents, or the former Administrators of the Territories – the latter surely men who are qualified to offer advice in the best interests of the native population. Under "Pang", the European residents will be little better than serfs – permitted to return only at the will of the Canberra clerks, without votes, without local government representation, and without even the right of having their laws submitted to the bar of public opinion.

MUTINY AT GROVELY

Below is a news item that somehow sneaked into the papers. Usually news of any sign of disaffection among our troops was quickly strangled at the source by our diligent censors. In this case, there must have been many civilians who knew about it, so that suppression was not possible. A small report was allowed into the papers. **There were no follow-up stories.**

News item. Australian soldiers under sentence tried to burn down part of Grovely army detention camp on Saturday night. Many shots were fired by the guards before the disturbance was quelled. The fire is understood to have been started after a futile attempt had been made by some of the soldiers to break out of camp.

Petrol was poured over a section of the grounds and was set ablaze. The fire brigade arrive at 1.15 a.m. and put out the fire. Some of the huts were badly damaged when a number of soldiers ransacked them. Army officers last night declined to make any statement.

STOP WORRYING ABOUT TICKS

Letters, Pluto, Wahroonga. The Education Department is quoted as pointing out the "danger from fleas on dogs, and hydatids and worms, and from septic dog bites." It may be reassuring to people who come in contact with dogs to know that only two canine diseases are transmissible to human beings – rabies and hydatids. Rabies is unknown in Australia. Hydatids can only be acquired by dogs having access to sheep offal, and this they cannot have unless they frequent slaughter places. They cannot transmit intestinal parasites to humans, neither do they transmit fleas. The dog is not a host for the human flea (Pulex irritans).

As for "septic dog bites," no sepsis need arise from a dog bite per se, since a dog's mouth (unlike a cat's mouth) is invariably clean. I have been associated with dogs for over fifty years, and during that time every veterinary surgeon with whom I have discussed these matters has endorsed these statements.

APRIL NEWS ITEMS

In the last 28 weeks, the Railway Department took **81 million gallons of water to Broken Hill in 900 water trains**. This was drought relief.

Retail fruitos will hold a mass meeting tomorrow to discuss **declaring apples "black"** unless the regulated price is raised.

News Item, April 6th. **Sleeping cars will re-appear on NSW Railways** from today. Some priorities **in bookings** for distance travel will be changed to **return some priorities to civilians**, rather than to the military….

News Item, April 8th. All **sleeping car reservations** for trains leaving Sydney for Melbourne and Brisbane **were booked out** yesterday.

The Federal Council of the Road Transport Union has decided to order members of the Union **to refuse to carry goods to and from establishments employing non-unionists.**

Restrictions have been eased by the Feds to allow the interstate **broadcast of 43 horse races per year in future**. Currently the number allowed is 19. Such races include the Melbourne Cup, the Caufield and Sydney Cups, the Grand National Steeple, the Epsom and Doncaster Handicaps, and the South Australian Derby.

On Friday, April 7th, **Russia told Japan that it would no longer be party to the Neutrality Pact** that had bound the two countries since 1941. In the quaint hypocritical world of diplomacy, this had meant the Russia would not take up arms against Japan, and indeed up till now, it had not done so….

By denouncing the Pact, **Russia was signalling to the Japanese that sometime soon Russia might attack Japan.** This was seen as a definite message to the Japanese population that **their war was lost.**

April 9th. US Army troops have stumbled on **Germany's entire gold reserve hidden in a salt mine.**

The former child star, **Shirley Temple,** who is now 16 years of age, **has announced her engagement** to a sergeant of the US Air Force. An engagement lasting two or three years is planned.

There was growing evidence that the **Churchill Government was losing its appeal to the people.** It turned out that this trend continued into the future, and at the next election, Churchill's Conservatives were tossed out. Churchill was a good war leader, but **not so popular in peace.**

The government is considering **lifting the restrictions on horse-racing information,** thus allowing the publication of Racing Guides in newspapers.

The **number of displaced people in Europe is now estimated at 7 million.** They are providing several difficulties to the Allied advance.

The **Commonwealth Disposals Commission has already sold many things to the public.** They include antiquated mosquito repellent, and ships under water. Also, **.303 rifles for pastoralists,** khaki shorts, one million yards of webbing elastic, and **seven hundred tons of ammunition.**

Premier Cosgrove of Tasmania announced that he plans to introduce legislation that bans the artificial insemination of women.

THE WRITING ON THE WALL

At the start of April, nothing was going Hitler's way. The Russians on the eastern and Balkans front had stolidly kept advancing, grinding down the German troops without mercy or hesitation. On the western front, the Americans, British and Canadians had galloped across the Rhine "like a nobbled greyhound", as one journalist put it. He meant that they were always going fast, but on occasions, they went very fast.

Most of Hitler's top generals wanted to surrender. After all, their armies were being beaten savagely, and their cities and industrial sites and railways and bridges were being obliterated by bombers every day and night. There was no glimmer of hope at all. Hitler, though, continued to talk about every soldier **fighting to the last bullet**, and refused to consider at all any talk about surrender. He was obsessed by the story of Frederick the Great, who once had a miraculous escape from a similar hopeless situation in the past. Maybe some act of fate, or of God, would come to his rescue. The odds were against it, but who knows.

With the Japanese, the situation looked much the same, except that in this theatre, events were a few months behind. But the same momentum was there. Japan's occupied territories were being reduced daily, and more and more cities were being bombed at the Allies' will. On top of that was the knowledge that after the **European** war was over, the Allies would speed their resources to **this** neck of the woods, and finish off the job post haste. It would have been a brave punter who bet against **that** happening.

So every day across this nation, people woke up to better and better news. The peace that people had been longing for, had been praying for, had been working and fighting for, was really possible. It might, or even it **would**, come soon, and that might be within a few weeks, or maybe in a few months. But it seemed that it was almost here, almost tangible, after five years of fear and loss and austerity. It was a time for hope and happiness.

PROBLEMS WITH GROG

Not so for everyone. The really sober men at the top were worried that Australia might start to celebrate too early. They knew that the Pacific war would keep on for quite a few months after the European, and that if Australia let up in its war efforts, then our victory might become uncertain again. So they were in a chorus, cautioning the nation about rejoicing in the European win, and telling anyone who would listen that **our** war needed as much effort as it ever had. Curtin, in a week of folly, even said he was considering closing hotels for **three days** across the nation when the European peace was announced, so that the enforced sobriety would ensure that our war effort was not diminished. He was backed up by dozens of clergymen who said that our population should go to church and celebrate with the congregation there.

Then Curtin came out and said that he was considering closing hotels on **Anzac Day as well.** It was part of his idea that production would suffer if we all got drunk. "My view is that Anzac Day should, as usual, be regarded as a symbolic day, not as a day of carnival, but one of reverence, during which Australians will show respect and gratitude for the men who fought and sacrificed.

"It will again be provided under National Security powers, as in 1942 to 1944, that hotels and wine salons will be closed all that day, that there will be no races held, and that pictures and theatres shall not open until after 1 pm."

His ideas were out of tune with most of the nation. **It** argued that, in the three previous years, we had accepted the restrictions on Anzac Day because we were still at risk of invasion. Now, however, when all such risk had disappeared it was pure wowserism to stop drinking on peace celebrations and Anzac Day. Everyone knew that Curtin was an ex-alcoholic, and that this often led to extreme views on boozing. Still they expected that their Prime Minister could rejoice along with them when the time was right. And that time was on Anzac Day and VE Day.

One lonely Letter-writer applauded Curtin's view.

Letters, F W Collins. As the father of sons engaged in action against the Japanese, I commend Mr Curtin for his courageous attitude. Since when has it been customary to celebrate victory halfway through a contest? Let us have our gatherings of thanksgiving by all means but Mr Curtin is right in warning against excess. We have to remember the starving millions of Europe and Asia who await relief and rehabilitation, and the prisoners of war still in Japanese hands.

Another put a different twist on it.

Letters, Ethel Vaughan Smith. All honour be to Mr Curtin, who has steered this country through one of the most difficult periods of its history, but – if he thinks that we are going to sit down and "gloom" when the cessation of hostilities against Germany is declared, he is not taking into consideration the basic qualities and characteristics of the British stock.

We are a disciplined but spiritually free people, and react in a healthy manner to any great emotional condition, be it joy or sorrow. British stock may be controlled but not regimented, and an emotional outlet is at times necessary.

A spokesman for the NSW RSL League said that the League protested emphatically against the Anzac Day decision. He said that it was only right that returned soldiers should have a drop of hard liquor with which to entertain friends whom they might see only once a year. It was a pretty tame show when a man got among his old cobbers and had to have coffee and biscuits.

He went on to suggest that ex-servicemen **only** should be allowed two pints (one and a half bottles) per person for their libations.

This raised the ire of non-servicemen.

> **Letters, Tommy Ball.** The suggestion that beer should be provided only for servicemen is offensive. I have been taken from my home and family for four years and made to work for the CCC in Central Australia. There are no home comforts in any location that I went to, and almost no leave. What the suggestion says is that the value of my work was nothing and not worthy of reward. I consider that I did as much for the war effort as anyone in the Services, and in fact, a lot more than most.

Generally, though, criticism was levelled at the whole concept of stopping people from celebrating on rare but significant days. The writer below spoke for many, in fact, most of the population.

> **Letters, Robt. Mitchell.** Cannot Mr Curtin visualise the probable reaction that will take place with the people of Australia when news is received that Germany is defeated? Does it not behove us to spread our hands spiritually across the sea to England – who bore the brunt of the day, who held the fort and saved Christianity for the world – to rejoice with them in their festivities?
>
> If days and days can be wasted in strikes, then let the people have their day for rejoicing. It would put new energy into our efforts to secure victory in the Pacific also, and would be the means of casting off those sombre cobwebs which have been hanging over us like a veil for the past five years.

Others had their say.

> **Letters, Grahame Bell.** Mr Curtin, in making his rulings concerning VE and Anzac days, has got the mood of the

country all wrong. We have listened to him for years, and have generally respected his requests for vast efforts. He himself must admit that our performance has been more than he asked for.

Now, at the end, he says we should restrain ourselves. We will want to celebrate on two days only. Not for a week or a month. We all know that half of our efforts are now wasted and that, for example, the bullets we produce will never be fired, and the roads we build will never be used.

It is time he stopped his nose-to-the-grindstone message, and stopped campaigning for the money for his next Commonwealth loan. If he persists, most of the population of this nation will ignore him and break the law on those two days. What good will this do for the country?

END OF FOUR LONG TERMS IN OFFICE

On April 13th, the US President, **Theodore Roosevelt died suddenly and unexpectedly** from heart problems. He was succeeded by Harry Truman who was, of course, another Democrat. Fortunately for the Allies, Truman was of much the same mind as his predecessor, and so he was able to smoothly continue on with existing polices and very small change of manpower.

This death was, nevertheless, a great loss for the Allies, and in particular the easy relationship and friendship that Roosevelt and Churchill had established would not be readily replicated. On the other hand, **Hitler saw it as the saving miracle that he had been longing for**. He hoped that the Allies would fall apart and start to squabble about the conduct of the war. In a few days, he realised that there was no hope of that happening under the firm, steady and reasonable hand of the new President.

IS THE WAR ENDING?

News from the battlefronts in Europe was coming thick and fast. In fact, too fast to be comprehended. It seemed to suggest that the war was almost at an end-point, and that perhaps some form of armistice would be achieved soon. Then again, maybe it was all just paper talk. Or maybe the German military could in fact give Hitler his miracle.

Of course, no one knew for sure. Every expert had his own opinion. I suggest we wait and see.

SHOPPING NEWS

I happen to know that things will get pretty hot in the next few months, so before that I thought I might give you some brief shopping news so that you would realise that the world was still going round, and that life in the suburbs was not as dour as you might think just reading all of my stuff.

My Son, My Son. "Why does it cost a small fortune to keep you in clothes?" That thought, of course, is only one of the highlights of being the mother of a strapping **lad** on the road to manhood. So we know we have the ears of such mothers when we tell them about these **sports coats** we ran down at David Jones'. It was the value that struck us. Only 15 – and 29 – (12 to 16 yrs. 6 and 12 coupons). Certainly ranges were broken, but every coat had the true DJ air about it, there were greys, fawns, browns, greens, and all were made ruggedly enough to defy any young man's powers of destruction. Youth Centre, 4th floor at DJ's.

Step further in Beauty Science. Whatever method of having **facial hairs removed** you've ever tried – Grace Manners wants you to try her new "Avaivo" Ray. It's as far in advance as the modern console radio is of the old cat's-whisker! She's so sure of its success that she'll welcome anyone to have a perfectly free sitting – and if you don't think it's absolutely painless and effective, you just walk out – there's no obligation. It's been examined by the Government and is fully approved. It takes half the time – half the number of sittings! Grace Manners, 3rd Floor, State Shopping Block, Market St. (M3182). Also over Miller and Curnows, Chatswood; 213 Church St. Parramatta; and 69 Hunter St. Newcastle.

Doesn't happen EVERY day! Certainly isn't often that you see **pantettes** at half coupon rating (which brings it down to a mere one coupon per pair!). The reason is that these at Winn's are actually slightly damaged – which makes the surprising price understandable too. They're really a find, in every way, because they're made with special shorter-length legs. The size is XOS and mostly women who need this size find the legs are made miles too long. But these ones are absolutely right – and of course, you save a coupon for every one you spend. They're 3/2 and just one coupon. At Winn's of Oxford St.

Underneath the Arches. The best thing to have underneath the arches these days is a pair of **comfy innersoles**. If you're not among the foot-happy, put 1/3 on a pair of these we discovered at Rigneys. They're a dual-season job and look very promising. One side they're Basil, a cool, thin, foot-caressing leather – (wear on hot day). The other they're warm, soothing felt for when the air's full of snow. Men AND women are both catered for – all sizes are there – and as we said 1/3 is little enough for all-the-year-round foot happiness.

OTHER REVEALING LETTERS

Letters, Anne Love. We had been told that ice was to be delivered without fail during the Easter holiday season, so, with confidence, we bought an adequate supply of meat, etc. but, in fact, we have not seen an ice cart for a week, with the result that we had to throw away half of our purchases, and also lose most of the milk and butter from our own cow. How much longer must housewives put up with such injustice?

Letters, W Robertson Brown. It is said that attempts to establish the mesquite here and there on the more or less empty pastoral spaces of Australia have not been successful. The results of trials by the Department of Agriculture have not been published nor have I observed reference to the mesquite in any agricultural journal or city newspaper.

And yet, in hot, arid northern India, in South Africa, Mexico, and southern California, altitude under 1,000 feet, climate Continental, shade temperature in summer rising to 100-113 degrees F, in the cold season at times dropping to 26 degrees, rainfall approximately 10 inches, I have seen areas of grand trees producing 200 to 300 lb or pods, closely resembling butter beans. Similar climatic conditions prevail over full one-third of all Australia. Even by the sea on the Hawaiian Islands, the mesquite grows and yields beans to the utmost perfection.

At this time of distress, when pastoralists are seeking something that may in future save their flocks from starvation, many would appreciate intimate detail of mesquite trials carried out by the Department of Agriculture. Some sheep stations may even have useful experience on the subject to relate.

Letters, N King. Pilfering from soldiers' parcels, and wholesale thieving of beer intended for the troops in New Guinea, seem to have been worse than usual before Christmas. Doubtless a large field for the black marketer exists here.

Here is an extract from a letter received from my brother, serving with the AIF. "We were paraded by our CO and told that we would not receive many of our Christmas parcels, and that thousands had been opened, and cigarettes and chocolates taken out. Also there would be no weekly issue of beer then, and for several weeks to come, as 60,000 bottles consigned to NG for us had been stolen at the wharves at Sydney. Our CO advised us to tell all our relations and friends when writing home, and ask them to advertise these facts as widely as possible, hoping that the matter might be taken up and something done about it."

Letters, Fiat Justitial. The death camps reported by the Allies are bad enough, but I refer you to what the Russians and others have suffered in the eastern front.

There the victims of German bestiality were numbered not in thousands but in millions. There every little village had its tale of horror, with its menfolk hung in the village square "pour encourager les autres," its women carried off to regimental brothels or to slave labour in the Reich. There mobile gas chambers toured the countryside and asphyxiated thousands whose only crime was that they were not Germans. The death-toll in Buchenwald is estimated at 60,000; at Kirkenau, in Poland, the figure was 1,750,000, and at Lublia 1,500,000; while in Odessa 23,000 Soviet citizens were herded into a barracks and burnt to death.

It might be recalled also that 250,000 Greeks starved to death under German rule. The score could be added to indefinitely. It is to be hoped that the Germans will be made to settle it in full.

TWO INTERESTING LETTERS

Letters, M Grant Cooper. A recent report in the "Herald" summarised a report by Lady Allen, chairman of the Nursery School Association in England, in which she commented upon cruelty in children's homes, one instance being **that meals are taken "in absolute silence."**

I am afraid that the majority of New South Wales charitable institutions for children could be indicted under this charge. I have been associated with various forms of welfare work for many years and have been an unhappy spectator on many occasions of the "silence at meals" rule, at which I have protested in vain. From the physical as well as the psychological aspect it must surely be bad. I have seen a large three-course meal consumed in about 12 minutes, this period including the service of the food!

Perhaps, now the matter has been brought to public attention, the committees of children's homes here will investigate the position and, I trust, rectify it.

Apart from children, I understand that a large public convalescent home for women insists on this rule.

Letters, A British Sailor.   May I express my deep appreciation of the unstinted kindness and sincere friendliness which I have experienced in Sydney during my short stay. The majority of us are civilians in uniform, doing a job, not because we like it, rather, that it has to be done. The rollicking beer-drinking bearded Jack Tar is the exception rather than the rule.

I have found the trees and flowers of Australia most interesting and absorbing. I have visited Sydney's fine shops, and browsed in the Mitchell Library, an edifice lofty and airy, and conducive to study. I had not known that contemporary painting was so good. Despite vivid flowers here and there, the main feature of her landscape is the gentle nuance of colouring, and it takes some little time to accustom the eye to it. Maybe **the brush** and not the pen will become the "forte" of Australia.

Politically and socially, I should say that the strikes and threats of strikes, the proposed control of banking and credit, exemplify the conditions obtaining in other free countries, where the destruction and frustration of war have but accelerated the desire for political, social and economic betterment. May it take a practical form in every country.

MAY NEWS ITEMS

Press reports indicate that **Mussolini begged for his life** with his lynch mob. His pleas were in vain.

Radio Station 2GB will broadcast **three news bulletins per day**, by arrangement with the Sydney Morning Herald.

News item, May 1ˢᵗ. The Prime Minister, **John Curtin, was admitted today to hospital** with congestion of the lungs. His Deputy will be Ben Chifley, probably.

The Premier of NSW said that the State **would not expect the people to refrain from rejoicing** when victory in Europe was announced.

May 8ᵗʰ News Item. Despite the threat of suspension, **4,000 unionists** employed by heavy industry at Port Kembla, **were absent from work yesterday to celebrate May Day.**

One thousand Army trucks will be released from the vehicle pool at Sydney's North Ryde Army depot.

5,000 skilled Brits are expected to arrive in Sydney soon to service the growing British fleet in Australian docks.

Newcastle wharf labourers have decided **to take a day off each week to search for tobacco** and cigarettes which they claim have disappeared from local tobacconists.

The transfer of dairy cattle from the drought area of the Riverina in Victoria was described as the **greatest mass-movement of cattle in the nation's history.**

Essential users of **horse-drawn vehicles** can draw **a special petrol ration** if the shortage of fodder makes this necessary. The Army announced that "**an accident occurred** to-day at an training centre at Wagga when 28 men were involved. Unfortunately, **24 of them were killed**, and four were seriously injured. No details are available at present." The SMH was able to establish that they were involved in bomb disposal work. **The Army, as usual, gave as little detail as possible.**

News report, May 25th. Fire brigades were kept busy last night **extinguishing Empire Day fires** in the streets of all capital cities. **Remember Cracker Night?**

The war in the Pacific continues. A typical news headline on May 28th. "The Japs lost 166 planes in **a series of suicide attacks against American shipping** and shore installations **at Okinawa.** Eleven American warships were damaged."

News item. In Britain, at the end of the war, the so-called national government cannot continue. This Ministry took the **best ministers from both sides of Parliament**, and thus made the best possible Cabinet for the prosecution of the war....

With the end of fighting, the rivalry of Party politics will be apparent again, and the old conflicts will re-emerge. This means that **Churchill** cannot guarantee the support he has had for the last five years, and so he **has announced that he will go to the polls for an election in a few months.** Australia, you will remember, did not form a national government, and fought the war with good doses of Party politics throughout.

A "bride" ship will leave Australia soon to take **400 Australian brides of American** servicemen to the US.

It is estimated that 125 million Europeans were short of clothing for last winter.

THE WAR IN EUROPE IS OVER

The British Ministry of Information announced that the German Army, now led by Admiral Doenitz, had been ordered to surrender unconditionally. The German Foreign Minister confirmed this, and said that "after almost six years of struggle, we have succumbed to the overwhelming power of our enemies."

Certain regions such as in Prague were stated as refusing to accept this. In such regions, heavy fighting continued but gradually the reluctant commanders accepted the truce, and their armies laid down their arms.

On May, 8th, after days of agonised wondering, the people of Britain were told that the war on the European continent was officially over, and that all combatants had ceased fighting. After five long, dreary and frightening years, it was finished, and to quote the immortal words of Vera Lynn, there will soon be blue birds over the white cliffs of Dover and, for the lucky ones, Jimmie will go to sleep in his own little room once more.

In the immediate aftermath, needless to say, scenes of revelry and debauchery were commonplace in Britain. They were widespread in Australia too, and no one seemed to be worrying about Curtain's exhortations to just get on with their jobs and stay sober. Of course, there were Church services a-plenty to thank God for this relief, and our leaders issued many profound and sincere messages intoning thanks for this divine blessing.

In the cities, the *SMH* reported that in Sydney, workers flooded Martin Place, shouting, waving flags, singing and laughing. Bars were rushed by the thirsty, who realised that to-morrow would supposedly be a dry day. *"Waltzing Matilda"* was sung over and over by any crowd who happened to gather. When they got too hoarse to sing, they wandered round waving flags and giving throaty cheers. People who initially intended to look on with austere amusement, found themselves caught up in it, and before they knew it, were linked arm-in-arm with men and women they had never seen in their lives, and were singing such songs as "Polly-wolly-doodle".

The *SMH* reported that Melbourne was more self-conscious, and celebrations there were almost forced. This does not fit with the many accounts I have had from readers who testify that it was a wow of a time. Also the *SMH* added, that in Sydney, there was little excessive drinking. Again, I can vouch that in a small coal-mining town called Abermain, excessive was hardly the word for it and, incidentally, it carried over into the next day, despite the official closure of the pubs.

Both Churchill and Roosevelt tempered their jubilation a little by reminding their peoples that the war with Japan was still ongoing, and it would take firm resolve to end it quickly.

OTHER EVENTS IN EUROPE

The month of May saw other major events in Europe. Notably, Hitler committed suicide before the surrender. His female partner, Eva Braun, was loyal to him to the last, and died at the same time. Goebbels and his wife died in the same bunker as Hitler, again by suicide, after his wife poisoned and killed their three children.

Most of the cities of Germany were bombed heavily in the final month. Berlin was virtually destroyed, and by the time the Russians and the Americans fully occupied that city, very little was left standing. Millions of German soldiers surrendered, and became prisoners-of-war, while at the same time, hundreds of thousands of Allies were released from captivity. As the Allied troops advanced, they discovered horror camps of starving people, including Jews, who had been imprisoned by the Nazis, and who now were barely surviving. **The photos from Belsen shocked the world.**

No one much was producing food, so hunger was rife right across Europe. By the same token, so much housing had been destroyed that again millions were living in desperate conditions. The medical and hospital facilities that were still operating were stretched beyond their limits. Chaos is the word that comes to mind except for the fact that it often implies a period of short duration. There was nothing short about this.

In the nations that Germany had earlier conquered, peace was still elusive. **In one scenario**, the patriot groups who had fought the Nazis were being pushed by the old regimes to give up their positions of power they had won at the end. For example, in Syria, the local freedom-fighters were now under military threat from the French who wanted to impose pre-war colonial conditions. So things were hotting up there. This however, did not please the British, so they had just landed troops there, and were on the point of entering the fighting **against the French**. What a way the start a peace.

In another scenario, the locals were confronted with their Russian liberators, who were intent on not going home. These latter set up their own military rule, and made all the moves that suggested that a Communist state was on the way. They also played dirty and serious tricks. For example, Poland had recently sent high-level delegates to so-called peace talks in Russia, but **these men were imprisoned**. I am reminded of the old question "Who needs enemies when you have friends like these?"

Comment. The happenings in Europe in this period have filled thousands of books since then, and I must desist from following them further **here**. After all, I am writing a social history of Australia, ten-twelve thousand miles away. On the other hand, this is what every Australian was reading about in their newspapers, and talking about, and listening to. For the month, the events of Europe were the stuff that all news was made of, and even events in the Pacific and Japan took a small back seat, even though they were momentous in themselves.

Further comment. I will use the available space in this Chapter to talk about other matters, and bring you up to date with the Pacific war in June.

STRIKES IN OZ: A NEW LEVEL

Had someone rung a bell? Was this the official start of the strike season? The answer is clearly "NO", because the strikes had been round for a long time. Now, however, since April, and into May, the incidence and severity had risen very sharply in the biggest Unions. The most logical reason was that, for three and a half years, they had listened to the distressed cries that said it was almost treason, almost sabotage, to go on strike when the national war effort needed every person's production. Most workers would say that the men in the Services should not be endangered by shortages of materials from home. So, for most of them, strikes were off the menu.

Things were different now. For months, the penny had been dropping that much of the nation's production was being wasted. If the Army Disposals stores were selling .303 bullets to the public, why work in factories to produce masses of them? If the Japs were now so far away, why build airports and build roads in god-forsaken parts of North Queensland? The last restraint on strikes went when it was definite that the war in Europe was over, and that **our** war was on its last legs.

So, strikes proliferated. The wharfies and miners, of course, went on as usual. But they were joined by bus and tram crews, factory workers both male and female, iron workers in all parts of that industry, bakers, butchers, milkmen, shearers, and you name them.

Not surprisingly, Letter-writers were very vocal.

Letters, W S Young. It seems ironical that when our politicians were giving their masterly exhibition, in Britain recently, of how to teach one's grandmother to suck eggs, they said sternly that the British home front could not slacken until Japan was beaten. Yet it is the strikes on our own home front that are holding up British ships operating in the Pacific war!

I wonder whether the work-weary, war-battered British people will be amused or irritated.

Letters, Spero Meliora. On Wednesday we celebrated the capitulation of the German forces, and in San Francisco representatives of the Allied Nations are endeavouring to formulate a policy that will prevent future wars.

Nearer at home however, in the State of New South Wales, peace and forbearance appear to have disappeared in the industrial field, and in their place we have anarchy and jungle law. The Governments, both Federal and State, either stand aloof, or, if one gives a timid direction, it finds itself ignored. Is there not someone strong enough to lead a crusade for the early establishment of industrial peace? We everyday members of the general public are caught, willy-nilly, in the maelstrom of these upheavals. We look to someone to whom we can turn; but look as we will, we can see no leader.

International peace may be coming, but what of the peace in our own fair land?

Letters, R Borthwick. The continued strikes throughout industry, particularly among the mining and waterfront workers, in such critical times as these, when our whole population is, or should be, fighting for its very existence, are extremely disquieting. It is a direct repudiation of the Government's promises to our allies (and this of course, means the people's promises) and particularly England and the promised industrial and docking assistance to her fleet.

In view of the serious nature of the effect on the war effort generally, and the repair of ships particularly, I think it would be an excellent idea if a petition could be arranged reprimanding these saboteurs. I feel sure that 85 to 90 per cent of Australians would welcome the opportunity so to attest their disgust. If something of the sort could be done, it would leave the workers and the authorities in no doubt as to the will of the people, and, further, what must be the demand of the people.

Letter, T Bailey. There is no doubt that employers for four years have hid behind national patriotism to force workers to accept bad conditions. For example, in my own coal mine, ten years ago a wing of the pit was closed down because it was unsafe from falls and dust. During the war, it was re-opened, and the miners said they would work it. **Only because of the national emergency.**

The same is true in all pits and all industries. Now, there is a backlog of claims that seek to reverse the conditions imposed and accepted because of the war. I hope that the bosses and owners will take a look at themselves and make the changes voluntarily. The alternative is to be faced with strike after strike for years, and in the long run they will be forced to make them anyway.

The same applies to the newspapers, including your own. Look at the cause of the strikes, and recognise that the causes are just, and that by continuing to condemn each and every strike, you are doing the nation and its citizens a major dis-service.

Comment. This sensible plea fell on deaf ears. Strikes continued to abound, and not one of them ever received the smallest degree of backing from the major dailies.

HOUSES FOR NO-ONE

When the war started, Governments big and small realised that resources for building new homes would become scarce, and one way to stop inequalities in the allocation of these resources was to stop building. So, between them they introduced laws and regulations and ordinances that virtually stopped all home building, and all land transactions, and all rent increases and all house repairs, until some time in the future. That future still had not come, and so by now there was still no home building worthy of mention. This was bad enough during the last forty months, but with the imminent return of a million people back to their old haunts, all looking for the bright future that they had been promised during their tours of duty, the housing shortage was rapidly becoming critical.

The governments had done a bit. They had recently set up their own Housing Commissions that had built estates to cater for dozens of applicants at a time. They had started various forms of lotteries, where lucky applicants could have their names drawn out of a hat to then buy a basic home. They had promised vast numbers of standard new dwellings in the future, and it seemed that they might be able to provide a small percentage of these. Steadfastly, however, they refused to allow private builders back into the market.

Letters, Sixth Divvy. The first thought of the married soldier is, naturally enough, to re-establish a home and resume life with his wife and children. Only a man who has experienced this long separation from his family can fully understand what it means. But such a course, at the present time is utterly impossible.

After eight months of civic life, I am still separated from my family. Until recently, I was unable to be with my wife, but was fortunate enough to secure a small flat, consisting of bedroom, kitchenette, and ten by four verandah. But my kiddies are still left out of the family circle. We are compelled to keep them at a boarding school (at a cost of over four pounds a week) because we are unable to find a home that will accommodate all of us. Nor is it for want of trying.

Those who stayed at home are still established in their homes. Thousands of refugees who poured into our country seem to have secured homes. But the ex-soldier and his family can sleep in the parks for all our grateful Government cares. There are thousands in the same predicament as myself. There will be thousands more before many more months have passed.

Letters, Mary Booth. The hopelessness of overtaking the housing shortage is obvious to everyone and is affecting the morale of the whole community. What could be done at once is to build hostels with apartments suitable for families of different sizes, with cafeteria and other essential domestic services attached. Such hostels could accommodate about 1,000 inmates (say 200 to 300 families). This plan was adopted in Italy during the re-housing period after the last war. The population of a given area would move into the hostel until their new homes were ready for occupation.

More recently there have been accounts of a similar hostel in a Welsh valley accommodating a thousand people, with cafeteria and other conveniences, in which a family could rent an apartment of three or four rooms at about 1 Pound per week. Good supervision would be necessary for the control of the establishment, and its location could be determined by local needs. This practical relief need not interfere with the housing plans already in hand.

Letters, Patriotic. Why not a campaign calling upon people as their contribution to the war effort to accommodate people without houses? I am sure room could be found in homes in the north shore and Vaucluse districts for people who are living under conditions that they never dreamed possible.

I have let a room in my home at a small rental – not for the purpose of making money – and I find it satisfactory I feel I have helped someone at a time when it was needed.

Letters, O C P. The answer to the suggestion from "Patriotic", that people with rooms to spare in their homes could help to relieve the housing shortage, is to be found in the Government regulations, which make it nearly impossible to get people out if they prove unsuitable, particularly if connected with the Services. Many people knowing this play up most unfairly, thus making it hard for decent people. I am in a position to know a lot of accommodation that would be available but for the fear of getting this type in. Thus, the regulations have the opposite effect to what is intended.

Comment. Even after private enterprise was allowed back in to the marketplace, much later, essential housing remained in short supply for decades. Wonderful new housing, shown in US magazines, just rubbed salt into the wounds.

LIQUOR FOR EX-SERVICEMENS' CLUBS

The Reverend Alan Walker was a rising star of the more conservative churches. The Methodist and Presbyterian Churches were well-known as being against any form of alcohol, and Walker was currently conducting a campaign against the rising threat that pub opening hours might be extended.

As a separate issue, a new menace was on his horizon. The number of ex-servicemen in society was increasing as more men were de-mobbed, and these men questioned the pre-war establishment. Why, they asked, could the Australian wealthy have clubs sprinkled discretely round Australia for the purpose of socialising, including drinking, while returned servicemen could not? Why could not the servicemen have their own clubs? This was the beginning of a campaign to make the formation of clubs of all sorts much easier.

Letters, P Messenger, Ex-Servicemen's Organisations, Randwick. Rev Mills Robson is reported in the "Herald" as having said: "The Church should protest strongly against the proposal to grant liquor licences to Servicemen's clubs."

If he had protested against the consumption of liquor generally and the licensing of any clubs at all it would be possible to understand his attitude, but why he should seek to prevent men who have fought for this country in two wars from enjoying the same privileges as are available to others, is a mystery to ex-Servicemen? It is to be preferred that the activities of members of these clubs should be under proper control, and surely Mr Robson will agree that it is far better that they should frequent their own clubs rather than seek their diversions in less reputable places.

More than 200 sub-branches of the RSL and other ex-Servicemen's organisations are solidly behind a committee formed 18 months ago for the purpose of securing licences. They believe that men who have served their country so well should be able to enjoy the privileges of club life which wealthier people are able to secure through membership of clubs which are already licensed. We rarely hear of any complaints about the clubs which at present have licences, and there is no reason to suspect that licensed returned soldiers' clubs would be managed and conducted in a less satisfactory manner.

JUNE NEWS ITEMS

The names of 165 more **Australians, released from German prison camps,** are included in the latest Army casualty list.

June 2nd. The acting Prime Minister, Ben Chifley, announced that **50,000 men would be released from the Services by Christmas.**

More than **3,300 war criminals,** including 3,085 Germans and 110 Italians, have **already been listed for trial** by the European War Crimes Commission. Many thousands of other war-time villains have been executed by lynch mobs as they surrendered.

There is strong support in the NSW Parliamentary Labour Party for **plans to establish** community hotels and to license **workingmens' and soldiers' clubs.** Remember when Workers' and RSL clubs did not exist?

A film crew arrived in Darwin to shoot scenes of a cattle trek for the film **"The Overlanders".**

The British, Americans, Russians and French **have divided Germany and Berlin into zones** that they each administer separately. London correspondents are concerned that these "zones of interest" **might harden unto permanent regions,** with strict boundaries between. **Question: How long did the Berlin Wall last?**

June 12th. **Gracie Fields** arrived **in Sydney** by plane today for a series of concerts in the Town Hall.

The Australian Council of Trade Unions has a conference every year. This year, hundreds of delegates from round

Australia will attend in Melbourne. **The Government has strong ties to the Unions.** It has arranged that three hotels will get **a special ration of 1,080 gallons of beer for them,** and a special tobacco allowance. **Not everyone is impressed.**

A shipload of **750 Australian prisoners-of-war,** the largest batch released so far, arrived in Sydney by sea this morning.

Losses of sheep because of the drought are estimated to total 20 million across the nation.

When young men were recruited to the RAAF, they were issued with standard gear **including two tin mugs.** Now that some are being discharged, **they are required to return** their standard issue, including the original mugs. **If they cannot do that, then their pay is being docked.**

A strike by theatre attendants at the industrial NSW city of **Newcastle** hit the news. It turned out that the Workers Union had guaranteed that it would not ask for wage increases during the war. They now considered that **the war** was over. **Do you think it was? ...**

The city and its suburbs **then had 18 movie theatres.** In 2015, it has three complexes and two theatres. **Things change.**

The Japanese strong-hold of **Okinawa was captured** by Americans late in the month. The Jap Commander **committed hara-kiri ceremoniously** on June 22nd. **Suicides among defeated military forces were on the increase.**

A Letters-writer railed against **doctors writing their prescriptions to chemists** in a mumbo-jumbo of distorted, English and Latin. **No one at that stage was questioning the requirement to write prescriptions in Latin.**

SOCIAL ISSUES AT HOME

The war in Europe was over. It took a while for the penny to drop, but by now it was really sinking in. All of a sudden, **people everywhere** were not worrying about what was happening in London, or Paris, or Berlin, but were thinking about what was happening to their families in their jobs and schools and own towns and cities. **The newspapers** found that about half their news-space was now available for folky news stories, and that sports news was still of interest, that stories about droughts and floods would always sell, and that scare tactics and outrages were just as news-worthy as before the war. **Letter-writers** got into the act, and enjoyed the much-increased freedom to hammer the various governments and authorities, and poured out a wonderful stream of complaints and mainly foolish suggestions.

For this month, there were three dominant themes.

SERVICE PREFERENCE

This was the idea that if a man spent his war years in the Armed Services, then when he returned from duty, he would get his old job back, or if he applied for a new job, then he would have preference over other applicants who had not served. There was also similar preference when it came to getting into vacant premises.

This sounds well and good, but when it put into practise, there were tons of problems. Was the man who served overseas to get priority over someone who had stayed in Oz? Was the man who served five years to be placed ahead of the man who had served for four? The men who had been conscripted to work in Oodnadatta for the CCC. Were they to be given full preference? Or none at all? Would a man who was clearly unqualified get a job instead of someone who was obviously perfect for the position? In housing, it was all similar. Would the man with no children get housing while a family of eight missed out?

The situation was further muddied because the Unions were at the same time urging for a similar **Union preference**. This time, the man with a Union ticket would get a house before someone without. The questions were endless and had many twists.

There were plenty of other cases. Let me illustrate with one example. Some airmen in England were shot down over enemy territory, and became POWs. Others remained safe, and stayed with their jobs, and in the normal course of events, were promoted. But these promotions were not available to the POWs. At the end of the war, when the men were receiving **deferred payments** for war service, the promoted men got more then those who were captured. Was this fair? It can be argued that had they not been captured, they too would have been promoted. In addition, it could be said that they had suffered more than their home-based counterparts, and should be paid **more**. These multitudinous questions were bedevilling all and sundry, and had no easy answer. **What would you have decided in the above case**?

At the moment, various Governments were in the process of legislating for servicemens' preference. There was much disagreement though, among the interested parties. Labour and Liberals had different and divided views, the RSL took a different tack, industry another, and so on. There was no clear-cut agreement, nor indeed, would there ever be.

SCHOOLS

Schools were back in the news. The complaints were of a general nature, with no specific news stirring writers into action. They signalled, however, that society was returning to normal, and that education was again something that was coming back as a matter for families to worry about.

Letters, Cicero. Everyone will agree with the call made by Mr Menzies recently for education to meet the problems of the new world. What are our schools doing?

My son is attending a good school, with a fine record, one of those schools to which we should look for our future leaders. This is the fare offered to him.

He learns parsing and analysis; this is called English: no literature of any sort is read or recommended. He learns and is asked to reproduce details of Acts of Parliament and political squabbles in England, hundreds of years ago: this is called history: it is not read with understanding, and the compulsion to memorise breaks any interest. No comparisons with modern times are made. Geography is taught well: thank God for that. Physics and chemistry are taught well, but nothing is heard of the biological sciences, which are of such urgent importance to our future in Australia.

The cataclysmic events of the present day are ignored. No mention has been made of the Atlantic Charter, the Yalta Conference, or San Francisco, while President Roosevelt died and was buried without a word.

As training for leisure, football and cricket serve: there is no music (except as an extra), beyond the roaring or squeaking of hymns at morning assembly, and no encouragement whatever of any handwork.

In a word, the curriculum and outlook of this school, which is one of the best, is identical with those of 50 years ago.

Letters, H W King, Canberra High School. Recently the Board of Secondary School Studies issued a new syllabus in geography for senior classes in secondary schools, and many have been the outcries of teachers and pupils in all parts of the State for textual material to meet it. With misguided enthusiasm I prepared a text-book which, in my opinion, as a practising teacher of many years standing, and in the opinion of several who might be deemed competent to express such an opinion, was capable of meeting those needs.

My publisher applied to the Book Sponsoring Committee for the release of a supply of suitable paper, other than newsprint. After some delay, the committee refused the publisher's application without giving any reason.

In the meantime, the material lies unused in the hands of the publisher, pupils and teachers are still endeavouring to garner material from sources which are very difficult to access in many cases, and clamouring for some assistance in that task, and the "unseen bureaucrats" continue on their bureaucratic way.

Letters, Australian Father. Cicero raises a question which must be present in every thinking Australian parent's mind. Is our education system adequate for the coming generation?

Why is so little attention given to (1) speech; (2) manners; (3) responsibility as citizens and founders of families? I suggest a full period in each day should be devoted (as one lesson) to these three questions.

It seems to me that a boy or girl is poor material for any sort of "new order" if – although crammed with academic knowledge – he or she (1) cannot speak decently; (2) is pitifully lacking in manners (vide many of our young people); and (3) has never been taught responsibility towards his fellow man in a civic and national sense. We cannot afford to leave this side of education to the home training and Sunday schools, however good these influences may be in certain cases.

FULL EMPLOYMENT

Doctor Evatt was a distinguished lawyer who had until now been a prominent figure in the Labour Party. He was one of those rare breed of politicians who combined a great intelligence with a high set of ideals, most of them too theoretical to be implemented. He was currently Australian Foreign Minister, and had recently achieved a level of prominence or notoriety for his work in setting up many aspects of the new United Nations organisation.

He was intent at the moment on establishing a **full employment policy in Australia**, and indeed, across the world via the UN. Everyone was quite happy with this ideal, but most were critical of his ability to actually implement it. In particular, most people saw it **as a way of socialising the nation**, arguing that the only way it could be done was for the Government to have control of all of the nation's resources.

A couple of writers have their say below.

Letters, E K White. At the moment our economy is akin to a jig-saw puzzle without a master diagram. Each pressure group, within and outside the Government, works for its own particular selfish end, and the devil take the hindermost.

Where is Australia's comprehensive plan of economy which sets out where the various parts fit and shows how we can progressively fulfil our national and international responsibilities as we go along? At present we all stumble along blindly. None of us, workers, employers, primary producers, manufacturers, or the nation itself, knows where we are going or when we will get there.

Everyone knows that our secondary industries have expanded during the war – but so have those of other nations. What are we going to do with our surplus products when the war-created local demand has been met? Perhaps some of the manufacturers who favour excessive tariffs will supply the answer. Until some sane and balanced solution to these problems is advanced, talk of full-time employment is impractical.

Letters, HUIE. Employment for everyone is a good idea. But will writing it into the United Nations' Charter be any more than a piece of specious window-dressing? It is eminently desirable that every man able and willing to work should have an opportunity to do so. If we consider for a moment the natural resources of Australia, or indeed of all the great countries of the world, there are ample opportunities for work. There is food to be produced, raw materials wanted, minerals to be won from the earth, and goods to be manufactured. Then there is all the transportation involved.

Has Dr Evatt anything else in view for the purpose of providing full employment? If so, he has kept it as a dark and fearsome secret to himself. Employment depends upon production from the country's natural resources. If these are freely available, and producers can freely exchange what they produce, there will be plenty of work and wages. To obtain this objective the host of restrictions upon the activities of the people must be removed. Other Allied countries have already made a good start. Why does Australia lag behind?

What harasses would-be home builders?   Restrictions. What stopped farmers growing wheat when they wanted to grow it? Restrictions. What prevents returned men getting living areas of land in this sparsely populated country? Restrictions due to bad laws. What stands in the way of legitimate business both internally and externally? Restrictions which favour some industries at the expense of other industries, which are naturally profitable. When did Dr Evatt show any disposition to help the ideal of full employment in a practical way by removing the multitude of restrictions which are lions in the path of work and wages for all.

Comment. Of course it is well known that, since then, Australia has had a low level of unemployment. Rarely has it approached 10 per cent, and has been generally about 4-6 per cent. This is very low by western standards. This happy state, however, did not come about because of any socialising moves along the Evatt lines, but because of the contrary efforts of a strong capitalist economy acting in conjunction with moderate governments. And, of course, just plain luck at times.

ATTITUDE TO THE GERMANS

The hatreds developed during the war are impossible to describe. Good, level-headed people, honestly going about their jobs at home, were confronted with the fact that their sons and friends were being killed and maimed and imprisoned by the Germans and Japs, and that there was nothing they could do about it. Their impotence turned to hatred, and if I call it red hatred you might just get some idea of its intensity. It was everywhere in society, and mellowed a little with the passage of time, but only a little bit at a time. **Even today**, it can be found in a few people, especially towards the Japs.

The following Letter shows some of this hatred. ˜Himmler had been chief of the Gestapo, and one of Hitler's top aides. Mr Tomholt spoke for very large numbers, and the hatred shown here was in no way restricted to him. As always, though, there was another slant on this matter, and writer L.J.L. also has his say. But his great opposition to Himmler and his Gestapo still came out.

Letters, Sydney Tomholt   Indignation must surely be universal at the cabled news this morning that the faith-denying mass-murderer, Himmler, received the last rites before his body was "lowered" – apparently reverently and not flung like that of his victims – into a nameless grave. This is, indeed, a gross insult to everyone professing Christian principles, but most of all to those 5,000,000 souls for whose slaughter Himmler has been officially credited.   The biting irony of it!   The butcher who so brutally denied the last rites to those he sent so savagely and sadistically to their deaths is himself given them by the very ones who should have indignantly refused them

– because they had first-hand and shocking evidence of his crimes.

Is the Himmler burial story but another indication that the world is once again to "go all soft" over those whom an instinctively healthy hatred should obliterate without a formal burial service? There are persons to whom the mention of hate is repugnant to their Christian principles. Let them see what Himmler was directly responsible for in the current and almost incredibly terrible film on the Nazi internment camp horrors. It is a historical document, a lesson for posterity, which makes the last rites for Himmler equally incredible and loathsome. It proves beyond doubt that mankind is entitled by its very Christianity to hate with all the passion at its command. If it does not, then God help Christianity and the future of mankind. For last rites then will be of little use.

Letters, L J L. Few will disagree with Sydney Tomholt in his disgust for the atrocities for which the fiendish Nazi, Himmler, was responsible, but many will fail to see any useful purpose or "Christianity" (the cause in which your correspondent writes), in his suggestion that the authorities in charge of Himmler's burial should have adopted the typical Nazi offensiveness of literally "flinging the body into the grave."

Could there be anything more futile than to attempt to take out revenge on the lifeless carcase of the man? A child fuming at some inanimate object has more to commend it, for the child is capable of investing the object with an element of responsibility which no thoughtful adult could possibly accord a dead body.

That Himmler, for his butchery, deserved the maximum punishment, I agree, and that would most certainly have been accorded him if he had not so cunningly cheated his captors of the opportunity. But if it is humiliation that is sought, what greater humiliation could be associated with his name than that, in full possession of his faculties, he took his own life rather than face trial for the consequences of his deeds?

OTHER MATTERS

I mentioned earlier that now that the war in Europe was over, the world's newspapers had more space for news not connected to the war. Happily, that applies to me as well, and so, right now, **I will indulge myself** by giving you a few diverse items chosen only because they interest me, and might do the same for you. In more relaxed years, I was able to find topics that I labelled "TRIVIA", and they lived up to that name. We have not yet got back to that happy state, but we are getting there.

Letters, Don Richardson. A report of the recent visit to Kosciusko of a Parliamentary Committee mentions the proposed building of "twenty small family chalets" in the vicinity of Smiggins's Holes. This would be a good start, but youth is ever charged with that spirit of adventure which will take him out on the main range and to the western faces, where the danger of being caught in bad weather, is ever present. And a man has to experience bad **main range** weather to appreciate the intensity of the elements which beset him.

I recollect a main range trip when six of us ran into early rain (September) with snow-proof but not rain-proof clothing. Visibility was reduced to a few feet at times and a high wind drove heavy rain into every part of our bodies. It was 12 miles between shelters, and when eventually we reached Pound's Creek hut, it was only with difficulty that we were able to remove our clothing. Only the uncanny sense of direction of the leader got us home.

Stockmen's huts are scattered over the main range, but the snow has no tracks and only the experienced main range skier can be sure of locating them, particularly in bad weather. Snow poles will lead a skier from the hotel to the Chalet (past Smiggins's Holes and Bett's Camp), but there are no poles on the main range.

Routes marked by snow poles would minimise the possibility of becoming lost.

No doubt the Government will heed the advice of Australia's skiing bodies), and so develop Australia's snowlands to the best advantage, adding yet another sport in which the youth of Australia can show its prowess to the world.

Letters, W S Edwards. The building industry needs assistance from engineers, technicians, and industrial chemists who have provided a number of synthetic materials which can be cheaply produced, and which do not possess the defects of present building materials. A modern house still consists of one-third timber in spite of all defects of wearing and shrinking. There is no reason why steel should not be used for joists and rafting in fibro-constructed houses. The whole frame, including the roof, could be of fabricated steel. During the twentieth century almost all the large industries have been reorganised, but with the building industry, one of the most important in the country, the position is otherwise.

Engineering mass production methods are essential if we are to lower costs. In the Ford Willow Run Factory, huge bombers came off the line at the rate of one per hour – why can't we organise the engineering industries of this country **to produce a house per hour**? It can be done if the resources were utilised to that objective.

Steps should be taken to modernise the brick and tile industries, which are 50 years behind the times. We should instal modern excavators and conveyors instead of picks and shovels and trucks pushed by man-power. We smile at the Arab's plough, but brickyards are just as ancient. Why do builders and Government authorities **insist on building houses to last three to four generations?** Compare the motor car of today with one 20 years ago. The engineers have given us a greatly improved car at a lower cost. The chaotic state of housing will not improve until modern engineering methods of production and planning are adopted right throughout the entirety of all the building industries.

JULY NEWS ITEMS

When the war in Europe started, **sporting matches between Britain and Australia were cancelled**. Now, however, a revival was underway, and an **Oz Services cricket team** was currently playing matches against the English Counties. The team included such post-war heroes such as Hassett, Pepper, Whitington, Keith Miller, and gradually recruited other players as they were stood down from active service in England. **It was ominous that a gentleman called Len Hutton was also playing for Yorkshire.**

Six persons were injured when a large trailer, carrying members and equipment of the **Tex Morton Rodeo Show**, was overturned at Jesmond near Newcastle in NSW.

The Japanese Army is still in control of China's Shanghai. It **has imprisoned 1,550 Germans living there**. Previously, when Germany was still fighting the Allies, they were valued friends for the Japs. **Now that Germany has surrendered**, Germans everywhere are seen as being part of the Allies camp, and thus are enemies of the Japanese State, even in Shanghai. **Life can be tricky.**

A bathing beauty contest, the United States versus Italy, is being held as part of the American Fourth of July celebrations. The contest is being staged in Rome between 25 American and 25 Italian girls. **The winner will be crowned "Miss Liberty,"** and the judging panel is weighted so that the US will win.

All reports of interviews with liberated war prisoners must be submitted for censorship, the Minister for Information, Arthur Calwell, said. Our censors never sleep.

The Chairman of the Victorian Housing Commission said

that the Commission was converting a **former tank-making factory for the mass production of concrete homes.**

Jewellers round the nation will soon **get a supply of Swiss watches for sale in their shops.** This will be because imports restrictions on them will be reduced. More alarm clocks from Canada will also be available.

The Government announced that the **number of coupons required to get many woollen goods would be reduced by about a third.** Apparently, more wool will be available now that the demands of the armed services have reduced.

Wearing up to six chevrons, 1,150 Army and Air Force **veterans returned to Sydney** on Saturday July 7th. More than half of them **were ex-prisoners of war repatriated from Germany.**

Fifty-two men from the military camp at Tamworth marched into town yesterday and complained about poor and inadequate food, and the punitive stoppage of dependents' allowances. **They then marched back to camp.**

News item, July 10th. **Total discharges** from the Armed Services in the last 18 months have been **130,000 men,** including 9,000 officers.

Within 20 months, an Australian-made car specifically designed for local needs is expected to be marketed **by General-Motors Holden.**

Housewives in Britain are campaigning for the removal of regulations and **customs that force them to queue.** In particular, they want to see **home deliveries (now banned) re-started**, remembering that most have no car, and no petrol. Australian housewives support this move here as well.

Here's an idea of the scale of this Pacific war: an official US estimate says that **27,000 Japanese aircraft have been shot down** so far.

Most of the Italians **held in prison camps** in Australia are working satisfactorily, but **the Germans are troublesome** and confined to their camps. The Minister for the Army said today that 17,700 Italians were held, and 1,567 Germans. **They were being held at the cost of the British government.** It was not yet decided when they would be returned to their own countries.

Surprise, Surprise. When the British election results were counted, **the Government of Mr Churchill was roundly defeated.** His number of seats fell from 376 to 165. The **Labour Party will form the new government, led by Clement Atlee.** In its election campaign, Labour had supported the idea of **socialisation of big industries.** This is in contrast to **Australia which had recently defeated the concept at a referendum**....

The Oz Labour government was blatantly ignoring this right now by "nationalising" or "socialising" the nation's airlines and "centralising" the banking system. These outrageous attempts to gain greater control over the wheels of business were **both eventually struck down** by the various referenda, and by Acts of the High Court.

The Prime Minister, Ben Chifley, has written to the States Premiers complaining **that the number of houses actually built in the last year was only 35 per cent of those promised**.

This question is being asked everywhere: **Will Russia now join the other Allies and declare war on Japan?**

WERE THE COMMOS BAD GUYS?

Communism was getting bad Press. Mind you, that was nothing new here in Australia because, from 1917, our capitalist Press had been strongly opposed to the birth of the new regime in Russia, and had joined with Australia's allies in doing everything possible to destroy the new Soviet. It was only half-way through the war that Russia switched over to the side of the Allies, and thereafter she suddenly became our friend, and her every action became admirable.

By July, the Germans were out of the war, and maybe – and maybe not – the Russians would stay on the side of the Allies, and declare war on Japan. **On the one hand**, she would have been mad if she didn't do this, because she would have then been in a position to claim the spoils of war for what should be only a few weeks contribution. **On the other**, her people were fed up with war, and had suffered worse that any other nation. Surely she should get out of the slaughter business, and send her troops home.

All of this left the average Australian on the horns of a dilemma. Should he persist with his open-arms togetherness approach to the Russians, or should he return to his previous attitude of deploring everything about them? At the moment, public commentary and the Press were leaning towards a return to vilification, but many womens' groups and others were still knitting beanies, and doing like things, for their armies.

Letters, Steve Crossley. The leaders of the Russian nation and the Russian army are the same leaders who are striving to promote Communism throughout the world. They aim to do it by bringing down the economies of many nations, and promoting revolution and seizure of property within them, and the killing of citizens.

We need to remember **that** when we think of our attitude the Russia. If we **did** get some help from them during the war, they did it for their own purposes, and not for ours. If they **do** enter the war against Japan, again it will be only for their own benefit. We owe them nothing for any of this. We should take the straight-forward attitude that we are different nations, but they are the ones who have their agents inside our nation, and those agents are trying to destroy our cherished ways of life. There is no room here for cuddles.

JOHN CURTIN'S DEATH

On Friday, 6th of July, the Acting Prime Minister announced that "the life of the Prime Minister, Mr John Curtin, came to an end peacefully and without pain in his sleep at 4am yesterday morning." After lying-in-waiting and a church service in King's Hall, Canberra, his body would be taken to Perth for burial. There was little fuss, just the honest tributes of hundreds of admirers and, a few days later, the election by the Labour Caucus of Ben Chifley as the new Prime Minister.

Comment one. I have talked to hundreds of people, from all political parties, and all walks of life, about John Curtin. Some of them agreed with his policies, and others disagreed violently. The one action above all that was most mentioned was his determination to bring Australia's forces home from Britain in the face of the strong opposition from Churchill and his ally, Roosevelt. Not one of them ever attacked the man, and indeed, all of them were full of praise for his qualities of industry, integrity, and far-sightedness.

Comment two. Frank Forde holds an unusual place in Australia's history. He was **Deputy** Prime Minister for a few months while Curtin was ailing. Then, for a week, he was **actual** Prime Minister until Chifley was elected. So, he held that exalted position **only for about a week.**

AUSTRALIA'S IMMIGRATION POLICY

As this nation turned away from the execution of the war, and towards the future, our extreme vulnerability to overseas conquest made us think about how we might increase the population. A number of public speakers were talking about recruiting families from Britain, and indeed a few of them were talking about simply shipping war-time orphans out to here.

There were other ideas though.

Letters, James Alexander. Our future policy must be planned so as not to disturb the friendly relations with our present allies. This particularly applies to the teeming millions of India and China, for with their awakening, the situation facing Australia's inadequate population will be truly alarming.

Mr Spooner deserves a Victoria Cross for his efforts to arouse us from our Rip van Winkle lethargy.

Letters, Jeff Bate, Legislative Assembly, Sydney. I look for an **alternative** to relaxing restrictions on alien immigration. Obviously, the two choicest ways of repopulating are our own babies and immigrants of British stock. Statistics show that rural districts are at present the great healthy reservoir of future population. From every 1,000 women at least 363 children under the age of five years are required even to maintain our present population. Rural areas produce 520 magnificent children per 1,000 women, provincial towns 420, and industrial areas 290.

Since the rural areas offer the most attractive employment for the British immigrant, how are they impressed by Australian conditions? My seven months attached to the British Army taught me that the average British reaction is that Australia is a land of drought, burning sands, and corrugated iron huts, lacking even the most primitive conveniences. What has New South Wales done to make country life attractive? Take vital water supply as an instance. Loan expenditure on water supplies, sewerage, and drainage in the last 87 years has been 28.6 million Pounds in the metropolitan area, and country towns a mere 4.7 million Pounds. Only a fraction has been spent on the country areas on vital amenities, electricity, transport, education, and hospitals.

Letters, V Davies. At last a few members of the community seem to realise the urgent need for immigration. But they seem to be aiming at the **wrong objective** – the lifting of the "White Australia" policy. They should be employing their energies to encourage white settlers. Now is the time to do something – when we have such a fine lot of boys from many countries, especially England, visiting our shores. Many of them are definitely interested in the prospects out here, and if we have a clearly laid down immigration policy, they will be able to make inquiries and really plan their future. The Government should immediately lay down a clear and helpful policy.

Letters, J A Hunter, The Manse, Haberfield. It is very disheartening to observe how political opponents seize onto points, and so overstress them as to ruin perspective. The simple fact of the matter is that we Australians must convince non-Europeans that our "white" Australia policy is not inspired at all by the Herrenvolk ideas we resented in the German attitude to the rest of the world.

Christians, who profess that Christ has broken down the middle wall of partition between race and race, may also recognise that there are economic and possibly other factors, too, which make it very undesirable to open the doors to indiscriminate immigration. But I feel safe in saying that among the factors in the Russian situation which commend themselves to Christians is first this: That there is no race-discrimination within the Union of Soviet Republics. Personally, I have some Chinese friends with respect to whom I feel no superiority in any sense.

I believe it could be arranged that a very small number of specially selected members of non-European races be permitted entry as a token of the principle that it is not mere race-difference which makes us discriminate; and we might well arrange for the presence amongst us of University students who would return to their own lands after their studies are completed. But always towards such strangers within our gates let us be courteous and kind.

Letters, R D Harrison. Mr Spender and Mr Thornton are to be congratulated on their international outlook on the white Australia policy, for it is one that not only concerns Australians but all white people everywhere. If we are to avoid great conflicts in the future between different classes and creeds, we must be prepared to share the living space, and Australia, with its vast undeveloped potentialities and varied climates, must be one of the first to make some contribution towards better living standards for the peoples of the world, whether black, brown, or yellow.

The problem for the present generation of Australians is to see that **the best types of coloured people only** are permitted to enjoy the advantages of living in a country developed and defended by white British subjects for more than 150 years. Many British and Allied peoples have earned this privilege, but it is for us to see that those permitted to migrate here are types that will carry on this development, and so make Australia nation truly representative of all that is best in human nature, irrespective of colour or creed.

Comment. As usual, some of these suggestions were sensible, and some were not. Notice that there were a few mentions of Asian migrants, but if you got the impression that Asians were scarcely welcome, you were spot on. In fact, with the Japanese now so hated by this nation, the tide against Asians generally was stronger than at any time in the past.

WAR IN THE PACIFIC

I will not try to describe the ruination that was descending on Japan. Just let me say that her forces everywhere were in retreat, and were being bombed by land, by sea and by air. Her cities were under constant air attack, and her coastal towns were being shelled by American ships off the coast. In short, the nation was being softened up by massively superior forces. It looked as though it might capitulate in the next few months, but the Japs were so fanatical about not losing that no one could tell.

The question was for how long could the Japs hold out. The prospect of having to fight the Jap forces **town by town, valley by valley**, over the whole country was a daunting one, and one the Allies were most reluctant to implement. Could they go on softening up the population over months until the entire Japanese economic system collapsed? **Or could there be some other way of breaking the looming deadlock? Would it be possible to break the Japanese resistance without the slaughter of Allied troops?**

FURTHER NOTE ON AUSTRALIAN FORCES

Sadly, Australians were **still** doing tough fighting, getting the Japs out of Pacific Islands and places like Borneo and even Malaya. There were many commentators who **now openly said** this was unnecessary because the Japs they were chasing were not going anywhere, and were now forgotten and isolated forces who could never get back into the war. Why not just leave them in isolation? Why have our own men killed for no gain at all? There was no easy answer to this, but one thing was certain. **The weekly lists of those killed and maimed still kept coming through, and these men and their families suffered just as much as those in 1942 had suffered.**

FOOD SHORTAGES IN BRITAIN

The Australian population was under tight rationing rules, and some foodstuffs and clothing and petrol consumption was a lot less that pre-war. But we were well off compared to the Brits. They had been on ever-decreasing rations since late 1939, and that was two years longer than we in Oz. Also, their per capita consumption was a lot lower than ours. On top of that, many imported goods were simply not available at all. For example, no bananas had entered Britain for the last four years.

Over the last year, Australians had started sending off parcels of goodies to their relatives and friends in Britain. **Over the next few years**, this would become more organised and be called the "Bundles for Britain" campaign, and huge amounts of supplies would be sent via that Government-backed scheme.

At the moment, though, well-wishers were privately using their own rations to create parcels for the Mother Country.

The first two Letters below give some idea of the processes involved.

> **Letters, Arthur J B Caradine.** Owing to the severe food rationing in England, I decided to help my sisters in London by sending a few parcels of foodstuffs, which I am given to understand are difficult to procure. The goods I sent were jam, mixed fruits, custard powder, currants and sweets.
>
> There is a limit in 3lb weight limit and the postal officials advise me it is only permissible to send one parcel per month to one address.
>
> Your readers will find that postage, packing, and insurance exceed the cost of the actual contents of the parcel! Furthermore, I find it is possible to send 11lb parcels of foodstuffs to almost any part of the world, excepting the United Kingdom.
>
> **Letters, W Bankes Amery, UK Food Mission to Australia.** With reference to Mr Caradine's letter in Tuesday's "Herald," most foodstuffs except bread, potatoes, and certain perishables are now tightly rationed in Britain, and successive Ministers of Food have decided in pursuance of the general principle that there **must be equal treatment**

for all, whether rich or poor, strong or weak, that food parcels weighing as much as 11lb cannot be admitted free of ration to people lucky enough to have friends in Australia, New Zealand, Canada, etc. As a **small personal concession to goodwill**, however, monthly 5lb parcels are admitted free of ration.

Hundreds of thousands of private 5lb food parcels now arrive in Britain from all parts of the English-speaking world, and they occupy shipping space which would otherwise be filled with bulk consignments of canned meat, canned or powdered milk, sugar, canned or dried fruit, and other foods urgently required for national distribution. There are such staggering shortages of food in the world today that it is considered more than ever essential to reserve supplies and shipping space for bulk distribution.

I believe that the most appreciated parcels are those containing solid meat, milk, tinned; jam, syrup, or honey, canned; or dried fruit; tinned dripping, and chocolate, with custard powder, jelly, or soap as a make weight. I do not consider it worth while to send ordinary boiled sweets as everyone in Britain gets a ration of 3oz of sweets weekly.

Letters, Where There's A Will. Would it be possible for certain city stores to allow women to buy, coupon-free, a warm garment of which they would not take personal delivery, but which would be handed in to the UNRRA or Salvation Army representative at that store? If that representative could sit at a table on the ground floor and give advice as to the garments most required, and have on display at her table clothing already purchased and donated, it would give additional stimulus and interest to a movement which I know would be welcomed by many.

MORE CLOTHING OPPORTUNITIES

Very rare; very desirable! When they told us over the telephone at Continental Bags that they had a beautiful bag of real Box calf leather – well, frankly we had to go round and see it with our own eyes before we were prepared to tell anyone else about it. But it's true. Only box calf could be so smooth, so sleek, so soft-and-firm both at the same time. Only box calf glows with the mellowness of old polished furniture. And because it IS box calf it won't ever lose its elegant slim flatness. It has a read good fastener, crepe lining, a little purse, a bright mirror, but somehow or other it's only 50/6. Continental Bags, 11 Imperial Arcade, or next to Angus and Robertson's, 87 Castlereagh St. (Mail Orders? Yes!)

Almost an Anachronism! Like something out of the dim and distant pre-war past, or something out of the glittering post-war world, shone upon our gaze this chromium-plated compact! Lovely to feel its ice-smooth 2½ inch expanse in our hands. Lovely to peer at ourselves in its clear, silvery mirror, set in the lid. Lovely to see again a frame of fine gauze to cover our favourite powder and sift it delicately through in just the right quantity. Lovely to get all this for just 10/6, at Angus and Coote's of 300 George St.

AUGUST NEWS ITEMS

The Federal Government announced that **private motorists would be entitled to a 20 percent increase in the petrol ration.** This would now allow about five short shopping tripsa month instead of the previous four....

Other changes included the removal of **gas-producer units from all taxis.** There would be no increase in the allowance for tyres.

A few days later, the Government announced that **the import of certain goods could now be resumed.** These included machinery for making matches and match-boxes, and for making paint. Also, gramophone needles, school chalks, and cream separators....

For the household, it now allowed the **importation of knives, fork and spoons, vacuum cleaners, tea-pots and soup bowls. All of these had been previously banned.** It would continue its ban on salmon and sardines. This was toensure that the Armed Forces had adequate supplies.

16 Japanese cities are now on the Allies' "death list". This was a warning to civilians that if they stayed in residence there, they would probably be bombed and killed. These were proving to be **no idle threats.**

August 7th. Washington announced that **an atom bomb, 2,000 times the power of any previous bomb, had been dropped on the Japanese city of Hiroshima.** The city had been destroyed. The Americans announced their intention **to drop more such bombs** if the Japanese did not **surrender unconditionally forthwith....**

The next day, the news media was flooded with opinions that the existence of atom bombs meant that **the end of the Japanese war was now imminent....**

Air-raids on Japanese cities continued in the days after the atom bomb....

Prime Minister Chifley said that he thought the war would continue for another year.

A Brisbane man was jailed for 14 days for **flogging his eight-year old son with a cat-o'-nine tails**. The boy had 17 weals on his back and buttocks. The cat originally had six leather straps, but three had been "worn away with use." There were eight children in the family, and all of them had earlier suffered similar lashings.

August 10. Surprise! Surprise! **Russia has announced that it is now at war with Japan**, and has invaded Japanese-held Manchuria. As one commentator put it, **the Russians were blown off the fence by the atom-bomb blast.**

News Item, August 10. A second atom bomb was dropped. This time on Nagasaki....

Further news on the Japanese war will be given in the body of this Chapter.

Would you like a bit of nostalgia? Do you remember when Mum brought some stewing steak, and some carrots and potatoes, and **slowly boiled them into a mush and served them up every Tuesday night?** With dough-boy floating there somewhere. **Solid, reliable Mum**, with home-made meat pies and an apple pie on Thursdays, **fish on Fridays**, and a Sunday lunch with a roast, followed by ice-cream and cakes for tea. **All home-cooked of course....**

Mums like that are hard to find today. So, too, I suspect, are families that would appreciate them....

But the other side of the coin is that bad days, like **Monday's washing days**, are also gone. And also Tuesday's **ironing day**. Good riddance. **Progress isn't all bad.**

DEATH THROES OF JAPAN'S EMPIRE

August 10th. The Allies specified that the Japanese surrender unconditionally. The Japanese, through their embassy in Switzerland, wanted to preserve some of the status of the Emperor.

August 12th**.** As the world waited breathlessly for Japan's reply to the Allies, Tokyo Radio called on the Japanese people "to await a call from the throne". This was a clear signal, coming from an authoritative source, that the Emperor would soon surrender unconditionally, and break the bad news to a despairing nation.

August 13th**.** The Japanese were uncertain. Were the Allies still planning to invade Japan? If they accepted the peace ultimatum, would it immediately end all hostilities?

August 14th**.** The Japanese surrendered with the preservation of the status of the Emperor as the only exception.

The surrender was accepted by the Allies, and the Japanese war was over.

August 15th**.** Australia celebrated in as orderly a manner as you would expect.

Comment. The war is over. Not maybe next week, not maybe tomorrow. There was no maybe about it. It was over. Australia had been on a war footing for three and a half years, and had been terrified for the first two of these. She had suffered the deaths and mutilation and torturing of her sons, had worked herself almost to dropping point, had lost her internal liberties, been rationed, and shunted all over the place.

That was all over. **Peace is here at last**. Celebrate, go to church, go to the pub, parade and dance in the street, sit and ponder the folly of war. Peace is special, and with it comes the **freedom** to do what you like.

SHOULD THE BOMB BE USED – EVER?

At the time, the Japanese did not know that America had used up all of its **two bombs, and there were no more in stock.** In any case though, more bombs were being made, and would soon be ready for use.

So, the war was over. Surely that would make everyone happy? Of course it did, **but** there were many who doubted whether the introduction of a new form of killing on a massive scale was acceptable, and where the world was headed. After the second A-bomb, at Nagasaki, it was obvious to all, right round the world, that such devastation had to stop.

Four clergymen wrote Letters to newspapers round the nation saying the bomb was a terrible instrument for the destruction of human lives, and its use was not in accordance with Christian beliefs. Controversy was really stirred up.

Letters, A V Robson (MSc), Sydney University. As a scientist, I can understand and appreciate the purport and possibilities of the atomic bomb. It is a further logical use of the resources of science and scientific manpower for a total war.

Its discovery and use serve to throw into bold relief the real nature of war in modern times, consisting as it does of annihilation on an unheard of scale, against which there is no defence at all, the guilty and innocent annihilated alike.

The use of the atomic bomb on crowded cities is not unlike bombing rabbits in a rabbit-warren, with no earthly chance of escape. It is comparable with Italy's bombing of the helpless Abyssinians not many years ago. Its use must inevitably produce, in the minds of those who live on, a hatred and enmity towards the United Nations, which will never be forgotten.

A way has been found at least of releasing the tremendous energy locked within the internal structure of the atom.

Drastic steps should be taken by the United Nations to control this discovery for the good of mankind not for its destruction.

Letters, Nemo. If the atomic bomb is treated as merely another weapon of war to be developed in secrecy by the military staffs of the various national states in the world, it is clear that the atmosphere of mistrust, suspicion, and fear which has existed in Europe since 1918 will be increased a thousandfold and spread across the whole world.

In such circumstances it seems certain that its discovery will lead to irreparable disaster.

Alternatively, we will have to recognise the fact that the atomic bomb together with the long-range rocket and the modern aeroplane, render the **idea of nationalism** as anachronistic as was the idea of the city-state after the advent of the stage coach and the sailing ship.

Probably no one really welcomes this new development, inescapable as it may have been in the circumstances. Those who will be able to regard it with some degree of satisfaction will be the individuals who hope that it will induce and compel the nations to sacrifice a measure of their sovereignty in the interests of a federated world government and a world police force.

Letters, M J Holmes. The Churches have always been ready to comply with requests from the King or the Government to hold days of prayer for victory or deliverance.

Would these same Churches now be willing to take the lead in organising a day of **national penitence** for the terrible use by the United Nations of those powers of nature which, in Churchill's words, have so long been mercifully withheld from the mind of man.

I feel this is the moment for the churches to lead us into new paths of peace and reconciliation, first pointing out the need for hearty repentance and amendment of life.

Letters, Tom D'Arcy-Irvine. The clergy are admired and respected by everyone in the community, irrespective of denomination, and their task is not easy.

The statement reported in the "Herald" on August 10 is difficult to reconcile when one continually reads and hears of authentic cases of Japanese atrocities and acts of outrageous conduct, descriptions of which cannot appear in print.

Referring to the moral right of the Allies to use the atomic bomb, Admiral Lord Louis Mountbatten is reported to have said he is in favour of it. He continued: "This war is crazy, but it would be crazier still if we accepted more casualties on our side to save Japanese lives."

Letters, I B White, Exeter. I wish to thank the three clergy of the Methodist Church who have protested against the use of the atomic bomb.

It has amazed and grieved me that those calling themselves Christian nations should by degrees become more and more barbarous. Surely it is time for those who really are trying to follow Christ to make their voices heard in protest against the continued use of this new horror. Scientists tell us that this new power can be used with great benefit in peaceful pursuits. Surely the knowledge was given to us for that purpose, not for destruction.

Letters, P Fraser Light. Many people are saying the atomic bomb is inhuman. Did they say the 50 or the 1,000 or 2,000 lb or 10 tons bombs were inhuman? At what weight did they consider the bomb to become inhuman?

Dropping the atomic bomb was the most humane act of either war. It saved countless lives and untold misery.

Letters, J A Levy. Surely those protesting against the use of the atomic bomb ought to thank Providence for placing this bomb **in Allied hands**. It has not only helped to finish the war quickly, saving millions of Pounds and the lives of all Allied soldiers, but possibly this new bomb may be used in peace to revolutionise everything.

Letters, Ruth Bedford. It would be understandable that such an idea as the atomic bomb should have emanated in Germany, but that great countries like the United States and Britain should be involved is a horror one can hardly bear to believe in.

I think every rational man and woman of every race and creed should band together and demand that this evil invention be destroyed.

Letters, R E Kennedy. If our Christian civilisation is anything more than a hollow mockery, the common peoples of the United Nations should speak up in protest against the atomic bombs. Christianity is the one faith that has always stressed the brotherhood of man, and the universal value of the human spirit, in whatever body it is housed. What a sight the "seared" areas of Japan must be in the eyes of Him

"Whose sad face from the Cross sees only this, After two thousand years."

Comment. Does the quotation have any relevance?

Letters, R R D. We cannot even imagine yet the extent of the barbarities practised on our soldiers and civilians who were unfortunate enough to fall into the hands of the merciless Japanese.

Do people generally picture the scene of defenceless men and women being bayoneted in cold blood?

We have the clergy protesting against the use of the atomic bomb on a nation devoid of pity. Is it any wonder that thinking people are drifting away from this stereotyped form of fanaticism which passes for religion?

Letters, L F Trevor. If the invention of the atomic bomb has at last shocked mankind into the realisation that modern war has indeed passed from being a medieval "sport of kings," hedged about with rules of etiquette and nice distinctions after the manner of the tournament, and has become total war of utter destruction, then we may hope that Governments will do their utmost to prevent war.

Of course, the weapon is a terrible weapon, but if the use of it compels Japan to yield and cease fighting, then its use is justified. We must weigh in the balance the loss of life of thousands of Allied troops if the war is prolonged for years against the loss of life of the Japanese if such destruction can make the rulers of Japan cease fighting in a few weeks.

In total war, can there actually be "civilians" when all, or nearly all, civilian activities are directed into war effort and factories make implements of war, and even children are employed in helping on the war?

Letters, J Chapple. The Methodist Church and clergy are protesting against the use of the atomic bomb.

From my point of view, the Church has, in this war, missed a wonderful opportunity, the greatest of all time. She does not understand the mind of the ordinary man. To me, the father of three sons in the fighting Services, anything that will speed victory is gladly welcomed by those who sorrow for those who will not return from the two world wars.

Comment one. There is no doubt that millions of Australians agreed with the last Letter. Why, they asked, would we kill off a single Australian just to save the lives of Japanese? Remember, at that time, this nation of ours saw the Japs as inhuman monsters, blood-thirsty, who had tried to enslave all Australia, and were now murdering and torturing our P-O-Ws. Who gives a hoot about the Japs.

Australia, still in the passion of war, would never have opted to **not** drop the bombs. **In a different time**, at a greater distance, more compassion might have been generated, and some consideration given to the horror of the slaughter of the humans at the bomb sites.

But this was not that time. Most of our citizens, myself as a lad included, rejoiced that the bombs had been so effective, and ignored the deaths, and also the longer term threats that obsessed the world for the next 30 years.

Comment two. At that time, the world was not aware of the **effects of radiation**. Even so, to say that the bomb had long-term destroyed twice the number of victims would have changed few minds, I suspect. In fact, in some quarters, such was the **climate of hatred, there would have been rejoicing.**

Comment three. I have almost finished writing these 27 books on the war years and the baby-boom years. **The volume of Letters on this topic was by far the greatest I have seen**. Every day for three weeks the Letters poured in.

This was not just true for my normal sources, like the *SMH* and the *Age*. It was true for morning and evening papers, right across the nation, from Brisbane to Perth, and from Hobart to Darwin. This is all the more remarkable given that most of them were written with pen and ink, and blotting paper.

OTHER PEACE NEWS

Part of the celebrations were victory parades in every city in Australia. Millions of people across this nation turned out either to march, or to line the route. Not just the armed services, but firemen, nurses, schools, ambulance men, Masons, Catholics, Miners' Lodges, wharfies, factory workers, anyone who felt like it. In Melbourne, a band of jockeys marched as a group.

In Sydney, one group who did **not** march were American servicemen. There was some confusion about this, but spokesmen said it was because they were not asked. This got some people vexed.

Letters, R M Mackay. One waited in vain to cheer an American unit in the Victory march.

An American officer told me, "We were all ready, but were not asked." If this be so, one is left wondering why so gallant an ally was ignored on such an occasion – an ally to whom Australia owes so much in men, material, and in spontaneous entertainment to our sons when in America.

Letters, Soldier's Mother. Mr Neagle's excuse is paltry. We have known for a week of the approach of peace. It was little use having a place in the procession for Americans and not telling them about it.

Letters, F S Burnell. The regret expressed by Mr J C Neagle, State president of the RSL that our American allies "did not know they were expected" to take part in Thursday's march, will certainly be shared by the majority of Australians.

Why did they not know? It is not enough to plead that the order of the march, as published in the Press, sufficiently indicated that they would have been welcome. Courtesy, to say nothing of gratitude, demanded that they should have been expressly invited. No such invitation apparently, was sent, and in consequence, our greatest ally, without whose timely aid all the heroism of our own fighting men would have been powerless to save us from the horrors of a Japanese invasion, was not represented by so much as a banner.

Letters, C E W Bean Through what was evidently some most unfortunate slip in the communications, the arrangements made for American participation in the Victory march miscarried, and Sydney missed the chance of expressing the depth of its appreciation of the comrades who came to us in our dark days, and of the great and friendly nation that sent them.

This will be regretted by nobody more than by our own returned men of both wars and by their British comrades.

The best way to make up for this lost opportunity will surely be to give us the first possible opportunity of expressing what we feel towards this very close and great ally and to all the men from overseas who have been with us and ours in this supreme test.

Letters, W R Bagnall. I suggest that steps be taken at once to organise a monster farewell to the magnificent soldiers, sailors, and airmen of our gallant ally, to take the form of Victory marches through the convenient cities and towns where American troops are quartered, to be followed by social celebrations in the respective town halls.

Let us do this in a big way and show our ally that Australians fully realise and appreciate their tremendous service.

Letters, Barry Cooper. The fact that US troops did not march was not naively because they were not asked. It was because they were playing politics at its best.

They have managed to put Australia on the back foot, with our politicians apologising to them, and our innocent public crying out for a special march just for them.

In the near future, when they enter peace talks, where they will divide up the spoils of war, they want every advantage they can get, and they foolishly think that such trivia will improve their position. Don't you worry about it, the great American Press will get hold of this story, and will use it to batter endlessly our representatives at the peace negotiations.

Do you think for a moment that the Yanks sat round waiting for the phone to ring, giving them an invitation to march? When the time expired, that they dropped a silent tear, and said "what a pity", and "that really hurt"?

Do you think that they are such delicate little violets that they would not have demanded to march if they really wanted to? Were they ever delicate with us at any stage of the war?

No, they can now sit and sulk, but be nobly hurt at the same time. A great win for America's non-stop diplomacy.

Letters, Crawford McKellar. At least the first day and the morning of the second Peace Day were splendid examples of a sober Sydney.

Surely the average citizen noticed the good-humour of the people, the peaceful streets, and what one might even call the beauty of the Domain when occupied by a happy, democratic people unsullied by drunkenness.

Surely, also, the average citizen then and there decided within himself that drunkenness and the indecencies that go with it are but another enemy within the nation – one deserving of as little tenderness as those other enemies but now brought down to unconditional surrender; or is it possible that this same average citizen is not prepared to stand up to the forces arrayed behind excessive drinking, or that he doubts at all but that yet another victory can be won by a united attack?

If we would look forward to a brave new world and all sorts of social reforms, here is one reform of high priority. Let then this same average citizen require of himself and of his Parliamentary representatives recognition of the fact that drunkenness is anti-social.

Letters, A N White. May I be permitted to make a suggestion in regard to the Sydney Cenotaph?

Now that the war is over I suggest the addition of four monuments – a nursing sister, airman, merchant Serviceman, and last, but by no means least, a fuzzy wuzzy. By this means we would be able to honour all branches of the Service and all those grand people who actually saw the war at its worst.

SEPTEMBER NEWS ITEMS

Prisoners of war were being released in all theatres of war. Thousands of Australian were freed, and the stories of **Japanese atrocities** were now being told....

Details were also emerging of terrible losses of Australian troops, as well as other Allied forces. For example, the death of 1,600 of our soldiers - **all of them prisoners of war -** some months earlier at Sandakan was revealed....

Occupation forces poured into Japan, while frantic efforts were made by the Allies to communicate with Japanese forces overseas to stop fighting. Many isolated **Japanese troops on far-flung islands, without radio contact, would not believe that the war was over**, and continued in their positions for months....

Of the 3,000 Australian men released from P-O-W camps in Singapore, none were fit to travel by normal troop-carrier ships. 1,000 will be sent on ships with a convalescent diet, and 2,000 will be flown home by air ambulance. Another 3,000 men died while in the camp. Lest we forget....

The first P-O-Ws to return to Sydney were packed into **double-decker buses**, suitably marked, and driven through the streets amid **cheering crowd**s.

Meanwhile, business in Australia had returned to normal. For example, Sydney was nearly crippled by **power strike**s that left it with severe electricity rationing. Also, the Americans were putting **pressure on the Brits to immediately start repaying the loans that had accumulated** under Lend-Lease during the war. **Life goes on.**

The inevitable was just starting. There were many islands and territories that were formerly classed as **Dutch colonies.**

These included the islands that now make up Indonesia. One of these, the large **Java, was already making determined noises about independence from foreign rule**. The desire to get rid of Dutch rule would grow quickly, and **similarly the French would be expelled from South East Asia** about fifteen and more years later.

The war was over, but industrial peace was a long way off. The number of strikers in NSW had reached 30,000, and other States showed similar figures. Miners' numbers were 10,000, iron workers 8,000, and waterside workers 4,000. All the big unions round the nation were on the warpath. There was no one now who could say that they were not patriotic. The war was over and they wanted different deals.

Five companies are competing to be allowed to build an Australian model car. These include Ford, Nuffield, Chrysler-Dodge, Rootes (Australia), and of course, Holden.

The Washington Daily News reported that **50,000 war brides (4,000 from Oz) are clamouring to enter America**. It says that "**American girls are wild with fury**, because they see that 50,000 of them will not find a mate" as a consequence.

A mechanical washing device, designed to assist **one-armed discharged ex-servicemen**, has been installed for the use of factory workers in a US city. It soaps, scrubs and rinses with practically no effort on the part of the user.

The Lord Mayor of Melbourne wants **hotels to be open until 10pm, and movie-theatres and "well-conducted dance halls" should be approved for Sundays.** He hopes that Melbourne will **bid successfully for the 1948 Olympic Games,** and fears that overseas tourists will get a bad impression if the current restrictions are still in place....

He was about twenty years ahead of his times.

NOW IT CAN BE TOLD

The newspapers and the air-waves were full of dreadful war stories that held the public spell-bound. Some of these stories had been known, but had been withheld by the censors because the Government did not want everyone to know. Others were information that was only now being discovered as the war ended and P-O-Ws were released. I have given you a mixed bag of six of these.

A DOCTOR HERO IN SIAM CAMP

News Item. The brilliant surgical skill of Lieutenant-Colonel Coates, formerly of the Royal Melbourne Hospital, was being acclaimed. Subsequently he became senior doctor with prisoners of war in Siam, working down the Bangkok-Moulmein railway, on the construction of which thousands died.

Coates used a sharpened teaspoon to scrape out tropical ulcers from the shinbones of hundreds of Australians' legs. The men bore up under the terrific pain while the doctor joked with them, often reciting poetry. He always had a cigarette for them after their ordeal.

With a Dutch chemist, Captain van Boxel, Coates worked feverishly, day and night, to concoct some form of anaesthetic to relieve the unbearable pain of **amputations**. After numerous experiments, they extracted alcohol from sake and wine and added cocaine received from the Japanese. They condensed the various fluids until they had a working spinal anaesthetic, so successful that they knew exactly how much to give for each minute it was desired to keep the patient under.

Many one-legged Australians here today, who call themselves "Coates's Boys," owe their lives to his skill and initiative and this vital discovery. Ingenious methods were applied to obtain gut for sutures. When possible, cows and other beasts were killed and gut extracted from their intestines.

Coates is now in charge of the main hospital in this city, where the troops are awaiting homeward-bound aircraft.

At one stage Coates and his orderlies were amputating at the rate of five a day among the railway construction gangs, so bad were the tropical ulcers. Altogether he performed about 500 operations. He says his patients were the pluckiest and most courageous any doctor ever had.

After some operations Coates would conduct a postmortem on the leg to prove gangrene had set in, and the patient would hobble over and join in the discussion. The boys made crude wooden legs of bamboo, on which they became remarkably adept.

SNAILS SAVED LIVES

Food in Changi camp was in short supply. The prisoners decided that they needed to supplement their rations. Several officers led the effort, and decided that growing pigs might help. But it was impossible to get food for them. They next tried hens, but the first batch of 300, bought from local Chinese, died from cholera. The second and third batch also suffered the same fate. **While they were alive, each P-O-W contributed two grains of rice from his daily ration to provide food for them.**

So, the officers turned to growing ducks, which proved immune to diseases. To feed them, every working party that left the camp **returned with buckets of snails each day**. They also organised collection points for food scraps to supplement the diet. The ducks thrived and, over the years, laid 47,000 eggs. According to medical officers, many desperately ill patients would not have survived but for these eggs.

A sentry was appointed each night to sleep with the ducks. But, according to Captain Ian McGregor of Toowoomba, who master-minded the venture, "only one egg was ever stolen, despite the fact that the men were always hungry."

SOME NURSES SURVIVED

News item. Twenty-four Australian nurses, only survivors of a party of 65, 29 of whom were bayoneted and machine-gunned by the Japanese on Banka Island in February, 1942, have been rescued from Sumatra. Found this morning, about 100 miles west of Palembang, they were flown to Singapore this afternoon.

The 65 nurses left Singapore just before the fortress fell in the auxiliary naval vessel Vyner Brooke, which was sunk by Japanese bombers in Banka Strait. Three of the nurses were drowned with many of the crew. A group of officers got ashore with the rest of the nurses, but ran into a Japanese patrol.

The Japanese took the naval officers off into the jungle and returned without them. They next marched a group of nurses into the water and bayoneted them in the back and machine-gunned them.

Staff Nurse Bullwinkel survived, falling into the water with bullet wounds in the shoulder and being left for dead. Crawling into the jungle, she wandered for several days before being again captured.

Escaping once again, she reached Java, where the Japanese found her working in a village hospital and tried to make her their officer Geisha girl. A German woman doctor in the same village made secret arrangements with friends and had her removed to another hospital in Bandoeng, where Murray met her and heard her story.

Sister Nesta James, Assistant Matron of the 10th AGH Singapore, 42, the senior of the party, said the nurses were suffering from malnutrition, and many from beri-beri and malaria. "The Japanese were tantalising," she said. "They did not strike or beat us, but practically starved us."

CHINESE CIVILIANS KILLED

News item. Forced by the Japanese in Singapore to drive their trucks, Driver C Barnier, of Grafton, NSW, had the gruesome task of taking Chinese civilians to their executioners, and watching their heads fall into the main street. The only Australian to witness the Japanese execution of civilians on a large scale, he will appear before a board in Sydney to give evidence on enemy atrocities.

"Five days after our capitulation, I was grabbed by the Japanese and forced to drive their trucks," he said. "At first the Japanese made me transport supplies. This was easy, and I began to think I had the most pleasant job in Singapore.

"One morning my Japanese guards told me I was required for a special job. Reporting to Japanese Headquarters, I was told to pick up some Chinese civilians and bring them to the court house. I found 10 pathetic, cowering Chinese women. A leering Japanese guard piled them into my truck and I took them to the court house. They were inside only a few minutes when I saw them driven out and forced into a broken-down hotel opposite.

"Through the swinging doorway of the hotel I saw Japanese guards raise their swords high. Then I saw the heads of these Chinese women roll out into the main street. Blood was everywhere. My stomach turned over, but I was powerless to prevent the incredible brutality."

Every morning he was forced to drive to some quarter of Singapore, pick up Chinese men and women and take them to the courthouse. After summary trial, the Chinese were promptly taken to the old hotel and executed. Often he was forced by the Japanese to drag out the bodies of dead Chinese civilians and take them away for cremation.

Large numbers of Japanese soldiers would gather outside the swinging door and cheer as the heads fell. Civilians who were starving to death were executed for stealing milk, food, or clothing.

It was a reign of terror. Between June and July, 1942, the Japanese cut the heads off 10 Indian and Chinese civilians, put them in his truck, and forced him to drive to the main business centre, where the heads were erected on poles. Underneath each head was placed a placard with the following inscription: "This may happen to you." The heads were left in position for 10 days.

Driver Barnier said he was then sent to Thailand to work on the notorious Thailand-Burmese railway. In his party, there were 3,000 British and Australian deaths from starvation and cholera. From 11pm until daylight on one night, he saw 37 men die. While working on the railway his weight fell from 11st 6lb to 5st 10lb.

BELSEN HORROR

Trials of war criminals in Europe were gathering pace. At the very end of the war, the Allies had found many camps where P-O-Ws were kept, and also a number of other concentration camps that held thousands of Jews and other displaced persons.

One of these was at Belsen in northern Germany, and at the end of the war, held 60,000 live prisoners. From 1942 to 1945, 20,000 Russian P-O-Ws died there and so too did 50,000 other inmates. When the camp was liberated by British and Canadian troops, **13,000 corpses were lying round the camp unburied.**

The war trials of Belsen guards were now beginning. The following is an excerpt from the opening address of a US Colonel Blackhouse.

News item. Backhouse told of locked huts so crowded with people that they could not lie down, and from which they could not move. He told of human bodies from which flesh had been cut and eaten by other humans. He told of women guards who found sport in setting wolfhounds to tear living people apart.

To the hushed Court, Backhouse described the gas chamber at Auschwitz, which had been used for the deliberate extermination of thousands, "probably millions," of human beings.

The Court would be shown a film taken by the British in Belsen, but, Backhouse said, "there are things a film cannot show. It can show you wretched prisoners scooping water out of a pool, but it cannot show you that the water was foul and thick with human bodies. A film can show you Belsen, but it cannot convey the indescribable smell."

Anticipating Kramer's defence that the horrors of Belsen were due to complete breakdown of the German supply organisation, Backhouse said it would be proved that at a military camp, less than a mile from the concentration, there were huge dumps of food. These included 600 tons of potatoes and 120 tons of tinned meat. At the military camp there was also a fully-staffed bakery with a daily capacity of 60,000 loaves, and large supplies of flour.

The British found dumps of medical supplies in the vicinity which were still not exhausted, although they had been used for the treatment of hundreds of thousands of prisoners.

Backhouse expressed the feeling of every allied national in the court when he said that the real horror was not the things he had been describing, but the fact that there existed in the German mind the determination to inflict these horrors on fellow human beings.

NAMES OF P-O-Ws.

As the Japanese military swept across the Pacific, they captured many prisoners of war, and set up camps in all sorts of places. Some were on Pacific Islands, some were in Burma, or in Java. In some cases, the prisoners were shipped to other locations so that they could be used there for slave labour. A number ended up on Japan's mainland, for example, in the most unlikely spot of Hokkaido, Japan's northern-most mainland island.

The Red Cross and the Army tried to find out where the captured troops were sent to, but this was an impossible task under wartime conditions. So there were thousands and thousands of prisoners who were being held, and our Army knew nothing of them. **Many of them had already been listed as Missing in Action** or as **Missing, Presumed Dead.**

As the Allied troops moved in across the entire Pacific and Japanese-held regions, the true size of the captured population became apparent, and it was obvious that **long-suffering families might suddenly have the hope that their loved one was still alive.**

The military was now flooded with the names of prisoners as they were released. They published these daily in the newspapers, hundreds at a time, and families were able to search each day for their missing soldier. Over time, the Army started to send telegrams to some, but this proved difficult to perfect. For most families, the newspaper remained the source they turned to.

The *SMH* added on each page. *"Because of the congestion on telephone lines and the possibility of error giving information by telephones, the Herald is unable to supply information by telephone about prisoners of war. The lists of names will be available at the O'Connell Street entrance to the Herald Office as soon as they are available."*

This system, though, had many faults. **Firstly**, the names were released in alphabetical order. That meant that if you were looking for Wilson, you had a month or more to wait. **Secondly**, if you lived a few miles away from the city, it was impossible to get to the O'Connell Street in your home city. So you had to wait for the paper to be delivered. Maybe an extra two days in remote locations.

Thirdly, by the time the lists got down to the M's, say, a lot of new names from earlier in the alphabet had been found. What to do with them? Sometimes they were added on to the alphabetical list. But that delayed`the alphabetical list. They system got increasingly chaotic as the total list grew longer.

But one thing was certain. Every name that did appear, and every one that did not appear, represented a real human. It might be a silly youth of eighteen, or a young man starting to seriously court, or an ambitious man in his twenties, or a father of three, or even a granddad or two. Everyone of these had mothers and fathers, siblings, children, wives and fiances, and others who were desperate for news of them.

This was a time of incredible agony for these good people as they looked every day, and possibly could not find, for the name they were seeking, and then had to wait till tomorrow. Would Dad be there tomorrow? Or the next day? The Army tried to speed up the release of names, but it had little control over their flow.

So amid the rejoicing to end the war, these families struggled on, sometimes for months, hoping often against hope, that their member would come home to them. **A sad, tragic scene**.

50 YEARS EARLIER

A Letter writer, a Mr Gordon-Hume, wrote a Letter that talked about how great life was 50 years ago. This Letter below, long and discursive, takes a different approach. You will find that it is obscure at times, and dripping with sarcasm, but I suggest you persevere, and enjoy the lesson in history.

> **Letters, M R Shannon.** "E Gordon-Hume's" remarks on what would have happened fifty years ago, with the spirited people of that time, stir up many vivid memories. **Those were the days!** No strikes then, except for the Great Maritime Strike which had paralysed coastal shipping for

many months, or the Great Shearing strike which had had Sydney in almost a state of siege, mounted patrols of "special" police parading streets in pairs with cavalry sabres hanging from saddle sides. Then, too, coal strikes in the Newcastle district did not usually occur more than once a month. No safety regulations in the mines and an explosion every once in so often were surely nothing for the Governments of the day to make a fuss about.

Public morality was at a very high level, except for trivial affairs of wholesale bribery to be later brought to light in the land scandals. A few highly placed men in public affairs were later to be prosecuted without much harm to them. Incidentally these men had all graduated into political life before the pernicious principle of payment of members had come into vogue. The old-time unpaid Parliamentarian was supposed to look after himself and very capably he managed it, thank you!

Fifty years ago, the Labour Party had but recently come into existence. The atmosphere of Parliament has never been quite the same since! The bank smashes were more or less in full swing. I was a depositor, so my memory is of actual experience. In due course, the customer was paid his money, or some of it. That was the case of the banks' **creditor** customers. That of the banks' **debtor** customers was another kettle of fish altogether. It was "every man for myself and God for us all," as the elephant said when he danced amongst the chickens.

In the happy days of fifty years ago all this **modern nonsense** about minimum wage, living wage, arbitration, rates of wages, hours of employment, etc., was not even dreamed of in polite society. It was freedom of contract then, and the wage-seeker had to accept what was offered. If a poor girl couldn't live on the wage, she was just out of luck. There were plenty more to take her place. The boy, so long as he was a boy, could get employment at a price, but when he reached manhood the order of the sack was his without asking for it. That is, if he expected a man's wages. I was one of them.

Elections were elections in those days. Where now do candidates tear each other limb from limb, as they did in the good old Free Trade against Protection elections, with yellow pup fighting green on the side lines? Where now can we find masters of political vituperation such as Johnny Norton, Jack McElhone, Paddy Crick?. All gone, now in these "spiritless" times, and along with them the steam tram, and the two-horse bus and one-horse hansom cab, and nothing now in their places but the spiritless electric tram, and the motor bus and the taxi. On occasion the old steam tram, with much jerking and puffing and letting-off of steam and coupler-rattling and bell-ringing, could do the full trip from Bent Street to Bondi Aquarium in one hour flat. Fifty years ago!

Those, indeed were the days. Nostalgia apart, perhaps we are better off with some later ones.

OCTOBER NEWS ITEMS

For more than three years, the Federal and States **Governments had cut the nation's racing industry to shreds.** They had reduced the number of race meetings in all venues to less than half, they had forbidden the broadcasting of most races, and they had decreed that **racing Form Guides were to be restricted to the point of being useless.** These Governments wanted the energy of the racing industry to be directed towards the war effort....

On Monday, October 1ˢᵗ, a holiday in Sydney, the *SMH* took much glee in saying that it **would publish today a full Form Guides to Sydney's races.** Regulations had changed, and punters were now welcome to bet and provide the government with loads of easy money....

This was great news for the racing industry, and was a welcome sign that the Churches and "wowsers" **would not be able to keep their foot on that industry for much longer.**

Servicemen will return home by ship. Tomorrow, Shaw Savill will deliver 146 P-O-Ws from Europe. Also HMS Vindas will bring 113 officers and 25 female internees from "the East." A few days later, 500 members of the RAAF from Burma (HMS Sontay)....

In the next four days, **3,483 ex-P-O-Ws from Japanese camps** will arrive in Sydney and Brisbane.

The world was in political turmoil. For example, **Indonesians** were striking en masse against Dutch rule, **Ceylon** was arguing for a new Constitution and freedom from Britain, **Russia and Hungary** were arguing over trade deals, the British Government announced that a new **Malayan Union** would be formed, **Siam** was losing control of its currency. **Everywhere you looked, turmoil and strife were evident,** and violence seemed to be the inevitable outcome in many places.

London, October 16. The Minister of Food announced that as a result of **increased supplies** from Australia and New Zealand, Britain's cheese and cooking fat ration would be restored on November 11th to **two ounces of fat instead of one, and three ounces of cheese instead of two per week.** Consumers can also now buy **three ounces of butter instead of two per week.**

General Gordon Bennett had been **commander of all Australian troops in Singapore up till the time of Japanese occupation.** In the night before the Japanese took control, **Bennett and a few officers escaped** in a small boat and made their way to Australia....

Many people claimed that he **had deserted his position** and his troops, while others said that **he brought back with him valuable information important for the execution of the war. Now,** Australian military authorities were preparing various charges that might be levelled at him, and preparing for his prosecution. **This matter would be played out in various tribunals over the next year.**

The United Nations has set up a system, UNRRA, whereby **food donations from many countries are pooled and then issued** to nations that are starving. **Japan** has now indicated that it **would like food from the pool** pending the harvesting of its next rice crop. **There were many who argued that Japan was not worthy of such a grant,** and should take the consequences.

The British Royal Navy in Australia has **stock piles of ammunition** that it no longer needs, including **many large shells.** They will be shipped to 20 miles off the coast of Sydney, and **dumped into no less than 300 feet of water.**

WHAT DID WE THINK OF THE JAPS?

There were already two very distinct schools of thought about how we should think about the Japs. **Firstly**, there were many, many people who had feared and hated the Japanese for years, and who were being reminded daily of their war-time atrocities. These people were being affronted constantly by the moderation being shown by the occupying American forces towards the Japanese, and were calling for tougher sanctions. I give you a sample of what they had to say.

Letters, L K MacKnight. The Press is full of accounts of the most bestial cruelty inflicted by the Japanese on our helpless prisoners of war, but no story could possibly equal in horror that of the massacre of 21 Australian nurses.

One can only wonder helplessly, why in the face of these records of unspeakable brutality, the forces in occupation of Japan **continue exercising such mild discipline over its native population**, particularly over its political and industrial leaders.

The **latitude and soft-heartedness** being displayed may, in some respects, be due to the fact that with few exceptions **the occupation forces are composed of troops who are fresh from the United States** and have had no personal experience in fighting the Japanese and certainly no experience as prisoners of war in their hands.

The only remedy would seem to be to invite volunteers from among recovered prisoners of war and soldiers **who have actually fought the Japanese and have first-hand knowledge of their treachery and cruelty to enlist for service as occupying troops.**

Letters, Constance A Murray, Pymble. What Australians are asking from their leaders is that everything should be done – and nothing left undone – to prevent the Japanese people from ever again wreaking their will on the peoples of the Pacific.

We and the Japanese are neighbours in the Pacific, and must try to live in harmony. Can such harmony ever exist until it is brought home to the hearts of the Japanese people – and war is made in the hearts of the people – that the qualities they have so far shown – aggression, treachery, and cruelty to an unparalleled degree – do not pay?

We are a peace-loving people, but we owe it to the future of our country for which our men and women have suffered and died at the hands of the Japanese people, that justice, and not pandering to Oriental psychology, be their lot.

Letters, Lest We Forget.   The earnest plea for a magnanimous tolerance towards our late enemies by some writers would appear to entirely disregard fundamental traits in the Japanese character.

These traits have been evidenced, first, by the barbaric cold-blooded ruthlessness with which the Oriental has waged the war, ignoring with it, almost totally, all humanitarian international agreements to which he had subscribed; and, secondly, by the remarkable volte face now exhibited by him in his smiling servility and his apparently sincere Press exhortations that a reasonable and just expiatory attitude should now be adopted by the people in atonement for their past misdeeds.

Should he now be allowed, with his ingrained Oriental treachery, to get away with it?

Until treachery and ingrained brutality can be exterminated from his fundamental make up, and he proved to be so, let our attitude towards him be governed in the light of our experiences. Intrinsic character traits are not to be changed in a day.

But there was a second school of thought. This was often based on Christianity, and it stressed that all humans were decent, that they have similar ideals and aspirations regardless of race, and that it was the propaganda spread by leaders that deceived the populace into supporting their evil schemes. From here it was argued that the Christian thing to do was to forgive and forget, and that the Japanese in future could be tamed by the good examples of Christians acting moderately and with compassion. The spokesperson for this approach was a lady called Janet Clunies-Ross, from a family well known on the Australian social scene. A typical Letter read:

> **Letters, Janet Clunies-Ross.** Justice can only be conceived and executed on a basis of calmness, logic, and knowledge, and even then must often be tempered with mercy to be effective. Justice can never be based on an attitude of blind fury, hate, and ignorance, which only breed fresh murder.
>
> I agree also that "pandering to Oriental psychology" is the last thing to be desired; but to deal effectively with any person or people one must know and understand a little of their background, education, and psychology.
>
> I agree also that "war is made (manufactured) in the hearts of the people," but by those in power, who rouse up evil passions by dishonest propaganda. The great majority of ordinary people in any nation are peace-loving, and hate war as much as we do.
>
> As for the atomic bomb, surely we can only be thankful that we did not need to make further use of such a terrible weapon – though it was only the horribly logical outcome of modern war, i.e., bigger and better bombs to kill and maim more and more humans in a shorter and shorter space of time.

She had her supporters.

> **Letters, Eleanor C Byrne,.** What is wrong with our white races? Have we lost all sense of proportion and common decency?
>
> Janet Clunies-Ross writes as a cultured, deep thinking, fair-minded human being. After six years of cruel,

relentless capitalistic slaughter, and she is subjected to the most bitter and blood-thirsty attacks from, in many cases, so-called Christians.

Letters, D L, Lindfield. I agree with Janet Clunies-Ross. I am unversed in international affairs, and know only that with all the brutality, vindictiveness, and hatred manifested at present it is comforting and encouraging to me to read so reasonable and compassionate an expression of thought.

I had been feeling that the hope of helping my little son, whose father was killed serving with the RAF, to reach a worthy and worthwhile manhood, could but end in sad disillusion, and that complete annihilation of humanity would be desirable – for what hope of happiness or goodness could there be with all hearts glorying in hatred?

But the letter from Mrs Clunies-Ross makes me believe there are many thousands in every land who feel as she does, and that humanity will one day be humane.

The *SMH* gave the Clunies-Ross opinion a good run in the Letters column. Other newspapers were not so generous. But the general populace were too set in their hatred to listen. Most of that populace were decent human beings, most of them espoused Christian values, and were quite prepared to give the rest of humanity a fair go. But it saw, at the moment, that the Japanese had earned themselves a place outside the normal bounds of humanity, and indeed were scarcely part of humanity. There was no way that, for the man and woman in the street, any amount of reasoning or cajoling was going to convince Australians that we should just get back to business as usual. The hatred was too deeply ingrained for that, and so the brief spurt of understanding and forbearance emanating from Clunies-Ross quickly made way for unbridled resentment and loathing.

Later Letters were universally condemnatory.

Letters, John Manton. Is it fair to these men and women who suffered hunger to return home and learn that Japanese prisoners in Australia are fed and cared for infinitely better than they were treated in Japan. If a small ration of rice was good enough for our soldiers in Japan, I consider the same ration should be meted out to Japanese prisoners in Australia.

Letters, (Mrs) D Clark. The inhuman cruelties and bestialities practised by the Japanese against prisoners of war were encouraged and ordered by highly placed, educated, and responsible officers. It is not a case of "forgive them for they know not what they do."

Letters, A A I. The Australian is not a revengeful or brutal foe, and is more likely to err on the side of generosity, but to put forward a plea that the Japanese is a poor, pitiable, ignorant animal is dangerous and absurd.

The Japanese must be rigorously punished. They should be excluded from the society of civilised people until they have proven their change of heart, and to change the heart of these barbarians is going to take a few generations.

Letters, H Landon Smith. I suggest that this would be best achieved by political leaders forthwith resolving to submit to the people a **referendum for debarment of Japanese subjects from entering Australia forever, and that this be written into the Constitution.**

If, while the Japanese mongrel practices are fresh in our minds, the opportunity is not taken to exclude them from our territories by means of our Constitution, as sure as night follows day, we shall see Japanese establishing **trade agencies in this country within the next decade or two.**

Comment. I scarcely need to remind my Australian readers that the feelings built up during the war were long-lasting, and it took a decade, or two decades, or three decades before many people were prepared to accept that the Japanese people should be accepted back into the human race. Indeed, there are still some of our living citizens, fortunately few in number, who will never accept them.

SOLDIERS' LAMENTS

Many soldiers were being de-mobbed. But many of them were still fighting the Japs in the fox-holes, or were baby-sitting Japanese POWs, or were maintaining peace in Indonesia, and South East Asia. Many of them were scheduled to return to be de-mobbed, but found often enough that shipping priorities had changed and that no ships could be found to bring them home. These war heroes were in danger of being forgotten.

Then, the following Letter caught the attention of the public.

> **Letters, Sixth Division, Wewak, New Guinea.** As from October 6, 20,000 men in the Wewak area have been living on half the normal food ration. For the past fortnight there has been no fresh food save bread (three slices a day), which is baked on the spot.
>
> All inquiries into this deplorable state of affairs fetch the same reply. A ship began loading on the 7th of last month and is still at the wharf.
>
> We have come to the stage when we rely mainly on vitamin pills for energy. More, we have now not only to feed ourselves, but an ever-increasing number of prisoners. **Who is responsible for this chaos?**
>
> The men here have been fighting, many of them for five years, to protect the liberties of their folk at home. From those folk, they expect at least food.
>
> When we left our native shores we placed our well-being in the hands of the people who remained. But now a large proportion of those people – an act of outright treachery – use the power placed in their hands by the exigencies of war to improve their conditions at home at the expense of the stomachs of those who have been fighting for them.

If such things go unchecked, if these union men continue to wield a power far out of proportion to their numbers, and use that power to the detriment of those who fought for them, it will need surely something far greater than the power of man to make our country fit to live in.

This is the country to which we long to return. We are disgusted by the policy of the unions and, above all, by the smug content of the mass of the people. At the very least, the 20,000 men living here amid disease and sweat ask of you a little food. **When are you going to act?**

The newspapers became alive with indignation. Mothers all over the country went into print in Letters Some signed them selves "Mother", "Indignant Mother", "Soldiers Wife", and the like, because of fear of reprisals from the authorities. But if their names were cooked up, their alarm was not. These Letters were published under the *SMH* banner "Forgotten Men in New Guinea."

Letters, Mary Harvey, Collaroy. A letter I have just received from my son, a member of the 6th Division, has given me quite a lot of anxiety, and I think it only right that their treatment should be ventilated.

I quote from his letter, "The food position here is very bad and, believe me, everybody is feeling very annoyed. We have been living on bully beef and M and V for several weeks, and, from today on, we are on half rations. We are issued with two vitamin pills a day to keep us going.

"I do not know whether the wharf lumpers or the Government is to blame, but the sooner we take care of them the better. Some of the battalions are now having two meals a day, but most units are given three small issues. This has been a very hard, long campaign, and, unfortunately, very costly in lives. The way the troops are being treated now is disgusting and disgraceful, and the sooner the people back home know it the better."

For more than four years, I, with many other mothers, have lived in a state of dread as to the fate of our boys. Now that the war is over, surely we can at least expect that our boys are having enough food to help them to re-establish their health as far as possible.

Letters, Soldier's Wife.   From my husband in New Guinea. "We seem to be forgotten by the authorities in Australia, as the food position is acute. We have had no fresh meat or vegetables for over a fortnight, and we were told last night by the 6th Division radio station that there is only one day's ration left on the island and no prospects of getting any until October 9 or 10. We have some fresh meat on today, but that was because it was flown to us.

"The authorities seem to have forgotten that there are some 14,000 or 15,000 Japanese prisoners up here that have to be fed, and that is where portion of our rations are going. It seems hard to be fighting them one day and then the next having to share your tucker with them.

"Probably after tomorrow we will be forced to use our operational rations. There is also a shortage of medical supplies and Atebrin, and if things don't hurry up I won't be surprised if quite a lot of us go down with malaria again."

Letters, Indignant Mother. This state of affairs has existed for some months, and now on account of lifting of censorship, we may hear about it.

Men who have escaped prison camps are patiently awaiting transport home. Surely the "powers that be" must find themselves interested.

The unions reacted with much indignation that they were accused of wrongdoing. They said the problem was caused by a shortage of shipping. This argument did not hold much water because, for example, shipping could be found to carry our own American war brides back to the US. Then again, the wharfies' union could hardly point to their pristine record of good citizenship when they were at this very moment **refusing to load ships to carry arms to our armed forces** in the Malaya and Borneo region. Their reason was that the arms would be used against the local Reds and **that**, of course, could not be tolerated.

Other arguments were advanced. Empty ships were going back past the New Guinea ports daily. Could not they be used? They certainly could **not** be so used. They had to run to a schedule, and any diversion would upset that schedule. Well, what about an airlift? The tonnage would not be much in military terms. Don't be silly. Where can the Air Force conjure up planes and men for such an operation? After all, they were releasing men and resources at as fast a rate as possible.

In other words it was a great stuff-up, and no one was prepared to do anything about it. This situation, of limited rations, lasted for a full month, and then things reverted to normal. But the whole sorry mess, **exposed for once in the full gaze of an incredulous public**, did nothing to enhance the reputation of the Army, the wharfies, or the Government. It added to the growing feeling that nobody was really in control, and that powerful elements in this society could do **whatever they liked** with impunity.

ZONING

Before war started, the normal household had perhaps two or three bakers who would home-deliver bread. The same applied to milk, and meat, and fruit and veg, and rabbits. The housewife could make a choice of which vendor she used. Early in the war, however, it was realised that this was very wasteful of resources with, say, three bakers covering the same route every day.

So, a system of zoning was introduced that said that a single vendor should be given a certain area, and only he could ply that route.

This was not popular with the housewife. It was a lottery that might end up with a baker who was rude or carless, or whatever. There is no doubt that as the war went on, many vendors were now secure in having a number of captive customers, and their standards of delivery dropped.

On the other hand, most of the sellers thought it was great. They had a guaranteed number of customers, and the prices of everything were fixed, so that they were certain of a fair level of income and profit.

Now that the war was over, housewives were anxious to improve the services they used. So they called for the end of **queueing**, and for **home deliveries** of vegetable and groceries purchased from shops to be allowed. Most of all, though, they wanted an end to **zoning**.

I will not dwell too much on the battle that ensued. There were obviously the forces of free enterprise **on the one hand**. **On the other**, there were the various vendors who did not want to lose the cosy control of their territory, or want to be thrown back into the harsh world of competition.

The end result was that zoning was gradually abolished. Slowly, over the nation, various areas were released from zoning, so that it became possible to pick your supplier.

I should mention that it is a little ironic that the next wave of progress saw home deliveries stopped altogether in most areas, and so instead of just the one supplier of bread, you had none. **More nostalgia.**

NOVEMBER NEWS ITEMS

What a mess in Indonesia. The locals want full independence, completely free from the Dutch. The Dutch want Indonesia to become a federated state, with limited independence, but still subject to Dutch laws, control, and rule. The British want places like Borneo to remain as colonies, but with gradual movement to self-rule....

For most of November, assassinations, reprisals, riots, destruction of large towns by armed forces, have been constant. Dr Soekarno has emerged as a moderate leader of the Indonesian, but with no control over the radicals, who are basically Red inspired. Our own radical trade unions support these latter radicals....

Don't fret over it. This is just **the start** of hostilities, and I happen to know that they will take about **five years** to get Indonesia to independence....

The strikes within Australia are another matter. I won't go into detail, but will just tell you that there were employers, employees, trade unions, Labour parties, Russian Communists, and non-Russian Communists, socialists, and heaps of others, and all of them want something or other....

The unionists want more money and a shorter working week. Employers don't like that. The pro-Russians want a revolution, the socialists want state control over most activities, etc, ...

Nothing new here, really. Though the strike tempo in November is fantastic. Twice in the last month the Prime Minister was used the big stick to settle matters down. So, things are quite normal only more so. **But, don't fret over this, either.** This is just **the start** of hostilities, and I happen to know that it will take, **not five years, but 50 years** or more to get to a better place.

Footwear, stocking, hats, handkerchiefs, socks, and knitted garments will become coupon-free from November 16th.

Residents of NSW will now receive one pound of sugar (per month) for each sugar coupon, **instead of the two pounds previously.** This is because coal strikes have reduced the capacity of the sugar refineries.

A large squad of police were engaged last night attempting to **recover eight 20-millimetre anti-aircraft shells "souvenired" from HMS ship**, Unicorn, berthed at Sydney's Pyrmont. It is believed that five boys might be responsible for their removal. The bombs have a highly sensitive fuse, and **they will explode and kill any persons near them.**

Shark repellent, developed to protect airmen forced down during the war, is **now being applied to safeguard swimmers** at Sydney's Northern beaches.

General Eisenhower has accepted a gift from the Scottish government. It is for the permanent use of a commodious flat in Culzean Castle, near Prestwick, on a cliff overlooking the Atlantic. The amenities include 2,000 acres "for shooting". He hopes to use it for the entertainment of British guests.

Motorists will be able to **buy tyres for their cars and bikes once again** in the New Year, as the supply of rubber resumes.

The first Australian War Trials to try Japanese war criminals opened at Moratai on November 30th.

New interest rates on **fixed deposits with banks** were announced. The interest for **a fixed deposit of one year will be 1 per cent**. Interest on deposits over 1,000 Pounds will be 1.5 per cent up to sums of 1,000 Pounds, and one per cent thereafter. **These rates are half the pre-war level.**

THE WORLD IS STILL GOING ROUND

The news as I have presented it over the last few months has been pretty grim. It was full of Japanese atrocities, atom bombs, fun in Indonesia, strikes and other sad stories. That, however, is only part of the picture. The population of Australia was doing more than focus on those disturbing matters, and was in fact starting to rejoice in all of the good things that come with peace.

It was, of course, hard to get away entirely from war-related matters, but it was good that a few consumer products had gone off the ration, that shop-owners and chain stores were talking about home delivery, that the Lord Mayor of Melbourne was keen on brightening up Sundays there, that horse-racing news was being broadcast again, that tyres would soon be available again for the kids' bikes, and that parks across the nation could again be used for the playing of bowls.

There were hundreds of things like this, each of them small in their own way, but it was a delight each day to find that some restriction had been lifted or that something long-almost-forgotten would soon be available in the shops.

So, it was safe to say that the population was thriving. They were still annoyed by the slowness of being de-mobbed, and by the shortage of housing, by the constant strikes, by the hopeless bumbling of their politicians, and by dozens of like complaints. In the long run, though, they were blinking at the light and realising that peace had really come, that their lot would quickly improve, and the faster they got on with resuming normal life, the better for all.

So men and women were mating at a furious rate, and starting a boom in families. They were changing jobs. Most of them said "never mind the job I had before the war", I want something new. They were starting to save to buy a house, much nicer than the one they had grown up in. They aspired to a car, a mortgage, a block of dirt in the suburbs, and soon a Hills Hoist to grace their backyard.

Above all they, consciously or otherwise, wanted to break with the drab, static, predictable life that they had seen their parents living in the 1930s. They wanted some excitement, they wanted to live a better life, and they wanted all the old pre-war taboos to be buried and forgotten.

So, if the last two Chapters have painted a solemn and even depressing picture, I would like you to measure them against the one I have hastily waxed on just now. In the long run, for all the hassles that the former picture presented, it is the hope and enthusiasm of the latter that did in fact win through.

FOOD FOR BRITAIN

About two years ago, it was obvious that our British forebears were suffering from a shortage of clothing and blankets and the like. At that stage, local municipalities across the nation appealed for any surplus of these products to be donated to a central pool, and the **Bundles for Britain** campaign was successfully launched. This saw hundreds of tons of clothing and materials sent to our cousins in Britain, and reportedly saved many lives.

In September this year, a new slant on this started to appear in the Press. Food was in short supply around the world, and much of Europe was suffering famine, and many in central Europe were actually dying of starvation. The Brits were badly off because their rations were cut to the bone, but at least they had a guaranteed ration. They would not starve, but they were a very hungry lot.

So, in September, agitation started here to create a Food for Britain Fund. By early November, the idea had caught on, and the question was not whether such a Fund or Scheme should be formed, but what was the best way to do it.

By July next year, it was in full operation. Lord Mayors and others provided local depots that accumulated tons of foodstuffs that were then sent to Britain. The Feds helped pay the cartage on this, and also with the distribution. Individuals could also send packets of food to their own relatives, again with the help of the Government. As with all schemes thought up and executed in a short time, there were plenty of problems, but the Scheme was overall a huge success, and millions of Brits were prepared to testify to this for decades.

Comment.   If there were millions of Brits who **benefited** from this scheme, there were also a million Australians who **contributed**. This was no Government-run charity. It came from a spontaneous desire in ordinary Australians to help out the Mother Country. For the next two years, ordinary Australians sent their food, sometimes their own rations, to the Brits, often on a regular basis, and paying for most of it from their own pockets.

This brings me to my point here. **Virtually no one, no Australian, had a single thought that Australia was in any way separate from Britain and the British Empire.** There were no republicans in sight. There was no talk of getting rid of the monarchy. The King and Queen were the visible sign of a link that bound us and them together, and made us suffer when they suffered, and when they were hungry, we were hungry. For this time at least, we here were all Brits in our own way, and I must admit, as a silly old bugger, that it was a world that I liked and now miss at times.

HOW WERE THE FARMERS GOING?

Farmers had suffered a tough time since the start of the war. Their main problem was that most of their able-bodied workers had been taken away and put into the Services or the CCC. Also, there was no new farming equipment, no way of getting repairs done to machinery, and no chance of any wire netting for fencing.

Farmers came in all sorts of sizes and sizes. Some were graziers of sheep, some were wheat farmers, some dairy, some market gardeners. Whatever they were, they faced similar problems. What did the future look like now that peace was here? I can't give you a full answer. All I can do is quote three Letters that show different sides of the issue.

Letters, E L Killen, President, Graziers' Association of NSW. The present wave of industrial disturbances and the threat of an extension of these troubles are causing grave disquiet and uncertainty among rural producers, to whom the community looks for foodstuffs and the nation for the great bulk of the exports on which our economy depends.

While the public may see how continued strikes at the abattoirs may cause grave losses to graziers and others associated with the grazing industry, they possibly do not realise how serious may be the effect on rural activities of continued hold-ups on the waterfront and in secondary industries.

The man on the land is in the same position as any other business man. Before he can consider risking his capital he must feel sure of reasonably stable conditions. The hazards of drought, disease, and falling prices are ever present, and he is willing to face them. But if, added to these, he is uncertain about the prospects of shearing his sheep, harvesting his crop, being able to rail his product, or ship it when it does arrive in Sydney, if he sees on every hand evidences of pressure tactics which must delay reconstruction and the expansion of markets, he can hardly consider himself justified in outlaying further capital on stock or in other desirable directions.

This, I suggest, is bad for the nation and for the individual citizen. The latter is still unable to get all the meat, butter, and other commodities he can consume and wants. Since it is to be hoped that our export trade will keep up, the only way in which these things can possibly be made available is by increased production. And increased production means increased outlay on the part of rural producers.

Until some stability is introduced into the field of industrial relations, and respect for the law becomes a real thing and not the mockery it is today, any real expansion of rural production will be hamstrung.

Letters, J J Collingwood. Your recent Leader on Land for ex-Servicemen was well timed. You state 60 per cent of the **soldier settlers** who went on the land after the last war have given up their farms. What of those who are left?

Many of them are burnt out, and asking themselves should they expect their sons, most of whom served in the recent war, to carry a similar burden.

After the First World War, I took up a block of land under the Soldier Settlement scheme. There were about 30 other settlers in the group, and they were decent, hard-working chaps. Few, however, are left; they never had a real chance.

The Soldier Settlement branch of the Lands Department was fair and considerate. It could recommend postponement of liabilities, wiping out of interest, etc., but this never got to the root of the trouble. This lay in the fact that the settler was never in a position to stand two consecutive bad years.

The selection of future soldier settlers should, therefore, be strict. Limited training on a Government farm is wasted, in my opinion, unless a man has had at least twelve months' practical experience of the type of work he intends following, he should not be permitted to take up land. The prospective settler will then have some idea of what is ahead of him.

Letters, L S Loewenthal. Without any sort of warning, all POW labour is to be withdrawn from primary producers in the Orange area after October 29. The POW and producers alike, because of the callous outlook of a few soap-box orators, are to be penalised. The primary producer is to be left the almost hopeless task of the harvest in a few weeks' time.

Australians have been horrified at the treatment that has been given to our own boys, but civilised peoples will be further horrified at the barbaric disregard for the rights of our own unfortunate prisoners of war. The bulk of these men, after about five years of servitude, are still only in their early twenties, and are practically all hand-picked for their honesty and decency and their sincerity to make good citizens, in spite of their baptism and enforced Fascism.

With very few exceptions they have done a good job for the nation. Most producers would have found it impossible to carry on without their help.

From a hiring fee of 2 Pounds a week, collected by the Control on behalf of the Receiver of Public Moneys, the prisoner of war is only allowed to retain the sum of 1/3 a day as a book entry. From this amount of 1/3 a day, the prisoner of war is permitted to purchase a few ounces of strictly rationed tobacco every three weeks from the Control Canteens, and also a few odds and ends.

On the food side of the question, a POW is also allowed the same ration as the Australian citizen, which is supplied by employers under strict military supervision. Clothing is made up of the torn and discarded uniforms of our own Services, and is dyed a vivid red. Hours of work are from 7.30am to 5.30pm, rain or shine. All public places of amusement are out of bounds.

Surely wiser counsels will permit these unfortunate boys to remain in employment with those employers who are capable of acting like human beings until such times as authority returns them to their own hearth and home.

Might I suggest that those disruptionists who state that **the POW is endangering their own competitive field of employment** could act fairly and squarely, and insist that the POW received an Australian wage if possible, or at least that he be returned at once to his homeland.

Comment. These Letters are just sideshows to the main game. For the bulk of farmers, until they could get their **sons and workers** back, and until they could get **the equipment they wanted**, they were just surviving. There was no miracle that would suddenly get them back, so all that could be done was to hang in there and hope that the wheels of national reconstruction would continue to turn.

HOW WERE HOUSEWIVES GOING?

At the start of the war, quite a few houses had some whiz-bang electrical appliances, like toasters, jugs and vacuum cleaners. Most houses, though, did not. In any case, by the time the war was over, all of these good things had given up the ghost, and there was no chance of getting them fixed. So, for the moment, but in the short term, households were forced to make do without these luxuries.

Still, with the end of the war, lots of women were losing their jobs in factories, and many of these did not want to join the ranks of the unemployed. So there was a pool of young female labour, eager to get work. At the same time, there was another group of female labour, with more money than ever before, who wanted someone to do their housework so that they could continue to work. Could the two sets of females come together for their mutual benefit?

Letters, Woman Medical Practitioner, Sydney. I read in the papers of the problem of unemployment of women caused by the closing down of factories engaged in war work. Why cannot these women find employment in domestic work?

It seems ridiculous, when harassed, war-weary mothers are calling out for domestic help, that women should be supported by the Government (and therefore by the tax-payers!) either by continuing these useless factories or by non-employment doles. **This lack of domestic help is a definite factor in the falling of our birthrate.**

Domestic help under a considerate employer is one for the healthiest of occupations. Good food, regular hours, and no mental strain, and a definite income with no deductions such as fares, lunches, and keep achieve this result. Mistresses will be more considerate now than formerly, and the helpers' status should be better.

This suggestion was met by a barrage of Letters that all said that young women were happy to do housekeeping provided that it did not involve washing, ironing, cooking, or gardening. Those who were prepared to live in wanted no duties after six at night, and no week-end work. **Above all, no children.**

Letters, Hopeful. Being the 28-year-old mother of four children under seven years old, I have for a long time tried to obtain some help in our home. I have answered numerous advertisements, always with the same reply, if any. **The advertiser will not consider working where there are young children.**

Letters, John Gladstone. Seeing that Australian single girls object to work in homes where there are children, it seems to me that we should allow young women with good reputation from all northern European countries, including Germany, to come to Australia to act as lady helps or maids to married people with families.

Most of them would get married, and their boys and girls would be 100 per cent "Aussies," and they in their turn could get young women to help from the countries whose women outnumber the men.

We would not let these women compete with our own girls in any other way, in view of the wonderful work our women and girls have done for us during the two World Wars.

Comment. It quickly became obvious that domestics, along the lines of pre-war Britain, would not become a major class of workers. There was no doubt about the demand, but the supply was not available.

HOW WERE OUR ANIMALS GOING?

Now that the war was over, the Government was making more newsprint available to newspapers. That meant that the skimpy little papers they had been publishing could now carry more news and features. So, for example, the *SMH* had recently added about four pages to its daily average. It also was reducing the number of war-time reports, and changing over to items with a non-military bent. **A good thing.**

One consequence of the latter move was that little paragraphs on animals started to re-appear in the *SMH* pages. For about two years, they had been virtually absent but now, at last, they were back again in all their splendour.

Letters, J D S. Three years ago the Army made an appeal for the loan of dogs suitable for Army duties, and I lent a valuable dog just 12 months old. On several occasions since I have tried to have news of my dog, but without success. Unofficially, I understand he was sent to New Guinea on duty. Now that the war is over the Army should return those dogs alive. The owners of those who died should be informed how they died – on service or from accident or sickness.

Letters, Disgusted Grocer. I am a retail grocer and have found great difficulty in maintaining a weekly delivery to my customers, not so much because of labour shortage, but shortage of motor tyres and horse feed. I have not been able to purchase a tyre for over three years, and have to beg for a bag of chaff once a fortnight to feed two horses.

I am wondering if all this is "fair dinkum," especially after reading that J Bendrodt set out for the Melbourne Cup with War Eagle. The animal is travelling in a one-horse float with two attendants. Bendrodt is trailing the float, accompanied by an assistant. Incidentally, the float is stacked with fodder. I wonder whether the tyres on the two vehicles will last the journey and what liquid fuel priority has a racehorse owner. It is a case of one law for the racehorses and another for the housewives who are forced to carry home their goods.

Letters, John Fisher, Bexley. It is to be deplored that on the day of the Melbourne Cup, a school broadcast was cancelled on the national stations. Whilst the principals and staff of our Public schools especially on Cup Day, try to keep down the gambling fever that has gripped the life of our children, the ABC makes the prowess of the animal pre-eminent over that of education.

Is the horse of more moral value than child life. Is the fever of gambling of greater value to the life of the future citizens of Australia than the broadcast of knowledge?

Letters, Jas Crawford, South Coast Pigeon Federation. The news that nine Army pigeons, tamed for their bravery during the war, have been returned to Australia for the purpose being killed, stuffed, and placed in a museum, has filled every pigeon and animal lover with dismay and disgust.

On behalf of the members of the South Coast Pigeon Federation, I wish to protest against such cold-blooded cruelty.

The British Government has awarded the Dickon Medal to many of its pigeon heroes; others have been placed on exhibition throughout England and have been viewed by some thousands of people. The reward of the Australian Army pigeons for their bravery is apparently to be death.

We are informed that these pigeons were instrumental in saving thousands of lives. If that be so, it is not too much to ask that they be allowed to retain theirs.

DECEMBER: CHRISTMAS THOUGHTS

Every time I finish a book, I indulge myself by writing about some of the memories or ideas that the year has brought to mind. So here I go again, this time pushing my luck fairly hard. You will find that I am a little blunter than normal, and if I get too far away from what you want, please forget it, and go on with the conclusion to this book.

By Christmas, 1945, I had reached the age of 11. I had two siblings living at home, and a good Mum and a good Dad that I loved dearly. We lived in a small coal-mining town of 2,000 people on the Cessnock coalfields, and 98 per cent of the men there worked in the pits. Many of them could scarcely read, some of them could scrawl their names. They lived in a closed society, travel outside the town was difficult with no cars and no petrol, and beer drinking and fighting in the pubs on Friday and Saturday night was just part of normal behaviour.

At this time, every one in the town was dead broke. Working in the pits paid a reasonable wage, but the miners collectively were always on strike, so often went from one fortnight to the next without any pay, so that living was always hand-to-mouth. This Christmas was particularly bad because they had followed the nearby Newcastle steelworkers out on strike for all November. Then they themselves had struck for most of December. So, the town was without pay-packets for the six weeks leading up to Christmas.

This raises a question in passing that I will address. Why go out on strike? If you needed the money, you had a history that said striking was useless, why not work and get paid?

The answer is the Reds, the Communists. They had control of the mining unions, and were intent on bringing the nation to its knees, and if they could stop the workers from working, they would be closer to bringing in their own idea of perfection.

So they called on the strikes. The rank-and-file miners were given the opportunity at times to vote on them, but they had a problem with this. If they voted **against** striking, then there were consequences in a closed town where everyone knew everything about everyone else. It turned out that the Reds had some friends who threw bricks through front windows of homes, who stole bikes from outside butchers' shops, who poisoned pet dogs with glass-baits, who bagged and drowned cats but returned their bodies, who bashed sons on the way to school. **The ultimate weapon was to brand a man a "scab".**

When a vote on a union matter was called, most miners stayed at home, and the Reds dictated policy. Thus, by Christmas Day 1945, the whole township was broke.

This brings me to my own memories of that Day. Mum had obviously been crying, and Dad too was clearly upset. They clucked us kids together and told us, with tears, that there was no money for presents this year, and all they could give each of us was a special commemorative florin that Mum had saved from the Canberra festivities in 1927.

We were all good kids. I suppose we were disappointed, but our main concern was to stop the parental tears. It took a while, not long, and life went on.

As I look back on this, I feel immense sadness that my parents were forced to do this. Those presents meant much, much more to them than they did to us. I feel sad too that this was just a part of the ongoing poverty that they lived with for most of their lives. It did not affect us kids, because we were loved, living in a happy home, and studying our way out of poverty. But, as I now appreciate, it was a huge burden on them. They would be pleased now to see that we, their children, have all moved well into the middle class and are fat and reasonably prosperous. I just wish that I could somehow share some of that prosperity with them.

HIT SONGS FOR 1945

Sentimental Journey	Doris Day
My Dreams are Getting Better	Doris Day
Rum and Coca Cola	Andrew Sisters
Till the End of Time	Perry Como
Dream	Frank Sinatra
I Can't Begin to tell You	Bing Crosby
It Might as well be Spring	Dick Haynes
Dig You Later	Perry Como
Bell Bottom Trousers	Jerry Colonna
Chickery Chick	Sammy Kaye
Doctor, Lawyer, Indian Chief	Betty Hutton
Ac-Cent-Tchu-Ate the Positive	W Herman
Feeling in the Moonlight	Perry Como
I'm Beginning to see the Light	Harry James
Temptation	Perry Como
There, I've Said it Again	Vaughan Monroe

US MOVIES

The Bells of St Mary's	Bing Crosby, Ingrid Bergman
Spellbound	Ingrid Bergman, Gregory Peck
Anchors Away	Gene Kelly, Frank Sinatra
Valley of Decision	Greer Garson, Gregory Peck
Wonder Man	Danny Kaye, Virginia Mayo
Lost Weekend	Ray Milland, Jane Wyman
The Dolly Sisters	Betty Grable, June Haver
A Tree Grows in Brooklyn	Dorothy McGuire, James Dunn
State Fair	Jeanne Crain, Dana Andrews
The Stork Club	Betty Hutton

THE STRIKES ARE OVER – FOR NOW

As I mentioned in passing above, miners in NSW were on strike for most of December. They went back to work just before Christmas, and the NSW Government made some changes to electricity power consumption regulations. I give you a few clues as to what they **had been.**

Under the headline, "MORE POWER CUTS EASED", and under the by-line "Breakfast may be cooked", the following news item appeared in the *SMH.*

> Restrictions on the domestic use of gas and electricity have further been relaxed from mid-night last night, says the Government.
>
> Meals may now be cooked during two 2-hour periods each day; a single light may now be kept burning until 11 p.m.; electric coppers and electric irons may now be used for two hours per week; and radios may now be turned on for four hours per day.

These generous allowances were only made for Christmas Day. After that, the restrictions were in force again, hopefully only till January 7th.

Electricity restrictions made life difficult for shoppers, because shops were not allowed to use electricity. Shoppers had to carry articles to the doorways of shops so that they could see them properly. A shop-lifter's delight.

SOME THOUGHTS ON DE-MOBBING

Getting out of the Services was not as easy as getting into them. Right now there were hundreds of thousands of Servicemen who were anxious to be de-mobilised, and every one of them thought that it was **he** who should be at the very top of the list. The Army came up with **a points system** that was very complicated, and impractical to the point of being useless, but it did provide some guidelines. For example, men who been in the Army for five years should be given preference, and so too should those who could get a letter from a farmer saying that he was needed on the farm. But the Army was recruited **in bulk**, and it moved round in bulk, and there was no easy way of picking a farmer out of a battalion in Burma to send him back to the farm in Oodnadatta. The points system did establish priorities, but fell down in practice.

Letters, M D Hay, Law School Comforts Fund. May I draw attention to a great hardship to a very deserving class of students under the Government's announced priority demobilisation for students wishing to resume University training?

The priority applies only to Servicemen "who have completed at least a year of a course" and therefore shuts out men who deserve particularly well of their country. These are students who enlisted in the first and second terms of 1940, who, after the fall of France, realised the deadly peril in which we all stood, and were intelligent and patriotic enough to enlist then instead of waiting to complete their first year's course.

These students have served over five years in the Navy and the Army in various parts of the world. Their claim for demobilisation is a far stronger one than those who served a far shorter time.

Probably there is not a very large class affected, but those who are should not be debarred from the demobilisation they have richly earned, and the right to continue the course interrupted in 1940 and 1941. It is to be hoped the Government will include these students in the demobilisation priority.

Comment. This was no small matter. It had become clear that the de-mobbing process would go on for a long time, and official estimates suggested that they would take a full year and beyond. As this news sank in to the forces overseas, it became a source of great discontent to the men and their families.

Letters, J Allen. Almost a month ago the "Herald" published a letter from me about the release of a soldier who is a cutter and tailor, with almost 200 points.

The release was requested in reply to a letter from the Supply Department, asking me to step-up production of men's suits, and whether I required any employees released from the Army.

I showed in my letter that the Man-Power authorities had refused to recommend the release. On the same day that the letter appeared in the "Herald", an officer from the Supply Department appeared in my factory. He indignantly wanted to know why I had written about the matter when they were doing all they could. He definitely assured me that the soldier would be released in a month. In fact, he was so sure that he would allow me to cut his throat if the soldier was not out in the month.

Today I received a letter from the Army regretting that they cannot release the soldier.

Could I cut the throat of the officer from the Supply Department now, or do I have to wait till Monday, when the month expires?

Letters, Sergeant, Labuan, NG. Wives, mothers, and sweethearts of Servicemen in Western Borneo should beware of building up false hopes on figures given recently by a Government spokesman of the number of men to be returned to Australia during December.

It is time the RSL took up the cause of "the forgotten men of Western Borneo" who, further away from Australia than any other large body of Australian troops, are languishing here in the Labuan area.

True, the five-year personnel have gone home, but as they were promised their discharge nearly seven months ago, regardless of the end of the war, this does not help any.

Another six hundred men have gone home on occupational grounds, but as we know that **only a fraction of such men honour the terms of their discharge, and go to the work for which they obtained release**, this does not help either. Rather the reverse. Nor is there any task for the men to do here.

A few hundred low priority troops and the civil administration unit created for the purpose could easily look after the area till normal conditions return. And so we sit here, with no work and inadequate facilities for sport and entertainment, and reflect bitterly that the Australian people don't give a hoot for us anyway.

SOLVING OUR DOLLAR PROBLEM

Australia had come out of the war with a shortage of American dollars. This is a complicated matter that I am not qualified to instruct you in. Sufficient to say that our ability to import all the things we needed from America was curtailed because of our shortage of dollars, and there was no **easy** way to get more by trading.

Below is a suggestion that might help. Granted, it might be complicated in practice, and it would hardly make a difference to the total sum we needed, but on the surface it seemed attractive, and there was a lot of support through the newspaper columns.

Letters, Rum and Coca Cola. Admittedly one of the most important things economically at the moment is the building up of Australian possession of American dollars.

Well, here is a suggestion. There are over 4,000 wives and nearly 2,000 to 3,000 fiancees who are trying to get to their husbands and loved ones in the US..

As the Queen Mary has been transferred to transport European war brides without too much fuss and bother, what about the Australian Government hiring a large ship, and transporting us? Most of us would be glad to pay the 100 to 150 Pounds required, and the Australian

Government, in accepting the job which American authorities are apparently unable to fulfil, could convert our money into American dollars. This should make everybody happy. Besides that – it would earn for Australia over 2 million dollars in a matter of weeks.

Any bride or fiancée would be glad to pay rather than be subject to continued disappointment, financial worry, and mental strain. The humiliating position of both wives and fiancees is unnecessarily ugly, and without dignity on the part of either Government.

WHAT TO GET FOR CHRISTMAS?

This year, I will point out some presents for the lady of the house. All of these are rather genteel, and perhaps you might instead decide that you want a new radio, or an electric food mixer, or perhaps one of these beaut new vacuum cleaners fresh from pre-war stock. In any case, these are all quite nice, and reflect the fact that the war is over, **but** that things are not yet back to normal.

All this luxury! If you always thought a fox fur cape was beyond the dreams of avarice, take a look at this one. It's a deep-piled, long-haired **fur** dyed to a richly dark brown. Yet it only costs 24 guineas, which you can see, puts it well within your reach. It fits close up to your throat, extending into wide shoulders. Very lovely over summer silks and evening gowns. And, of course, no one can forget these days that Christmas is coming! The place we spotted this cape is Sam Press . And it's 24 guineas, 5 coupons. Phone MJ4207.

Pinking Machine Here! Here's a Christmas Box of news for you professional and or advanced home dressmakers. A simple little **pinking machine**, that replaces the clumsy, old pinking shears (that have been unprocurable for donkeys' ages anyway).... Quite compact, occupies less than a foot of space, screws handily to the table, and by the turn of a handle, treats your materials to that very neat professional pinked finish that eliminates all fraying of seams of edges. David Jones' have this little wonder worker, or rather WILL have it. You'll have to wait till about next Thursday to buy one, but you can see the sample we saw at work on the Ground Floor, Main Store, now.

Satin, and long-sleeved! If one of your chief tea-table conversation-pieces is how you've searched all over town for a **long-sleeved satin blouse**, your conversation will be flat now. Because your search is over. We've found a lovely one for you at Chatterton's. Shimmery ivory satin, in the sweetest style, and the very divinest of long full sleeves. We thought it looked like at least three guineas, but the actual price is 41/9. Plus 7 coupons, in SSW, SW, W. And if you want something short-sleeved for a suit, also in shining satin, they have the loveliest pastel tints in a shirt-neckline style. At Chatterton's, 78 Castlereagh St.

Baby's Bath is ready! You'll welcome the sight of this **bath**, as you'd welcome an old friend – it's exactly the same as the baths were in those "good old days" before the war. The same rolled edge for getting a grip on, the same pretty nursery-pastels of pink, cream and green, and the same funny little baby-transfers to amuse the tiny occupant. People have been asking and asking about these particular baths, so we feel pleased to tell you that they're now a-plenty at Winn's of Oxford St. The price is 10/6, and it's a good notion to give someone who's expecting a baby some time after Christmas!

With the reduced coupon-rate, for woollen dress materials did you say, "Oh, yes, all very well for winter, but I want some new summer things?" For you then, we found at Kin-Sella **Silks the perfect material**. Think of it – it's 54 inches wide, and only 2 coupons a yard! The fabric is actually 100% wool, but it's one of those wonderfully fine weaves, created for summer, that we've all read about. It's meant for summer frocks, suits, coats, and looks very distinguished, too. All good colours.

A Perm as a Present. We're all excited over the idea of giving someone the Christmas present of **a Perm**. It's something every woman from sixteen to sixty would adore, and that she'd remember you for months. But, of course, not just any perm would do, and it would want to be at a rather special sort of salon, so, we thought that an "Ondulux" at Borrowman's would make a very good combination. Good idea for mothers to give teen-agers their first perm. Ask all about it. At Barrowman.

SUMMING UP 1945

At the start of the year, the world was at war. At the finish, it was not. That sums it up. Anyone could complain at this time about the Australian world, and find oodles of examples of things that were wrong. I have spent the last half of the book pointing out that strikes, inequities in the military, and hunger throughout the world were making life hard for millions of people, here and overseas. But no sane person could prefer the world of January 1945 to the world of December 1945, and to that extent, we can say that 1945 was a great year.

That is not to diminish the misery that millions suffered. Loss of life and property, the wholesale destruction of homes and jobs and dreams, the destruction of whole societies, these were the legacy of a bitter and protracted war. No one could pretend that the pain would go away quickly, or ever in fact. Some people might say that without the war, certain scientific facts might have lain dormant for years, or that some old and creaking institutions would have kept their firm hand on the multitudes. They are, of course, correct, but these advantages were so small relative to the immense losses as to not ascend beyond the insignificant.

I invite you to look **at a brief summary of the year**, and ask you as I do so to keep an eye on this question: Has there ever, **in Australia's history**, been a period of more rapid change for the entire society than in this year? Has there ever been more rapid change in **the history of the world**?

So, now the summary. I will just pick the eyes out of history, not always in the chronological order. The President of the US died. The Prime Minister of Australia died. Adolf Hitler committed suicide. The Battle of the Bulge left Germany without hope. The Russians and Allies and Yanks reduced German cities to rubbles. The Japs were cornered at home. America destroyed Japanese resistance with two atom bombs. Germany surrendered unconditionally. The Japs surrendered unconditionally.

These events came one after the other, each of them of immense significance, at a furious pace. All I can say is that when I hear people **today** complain about the pace of change being too rapid, I look away and try not to look knowing.

This leaves us, at the end of 1945, with a clean slate. Well, perhaps it is not quite clean. Perhaps in fact, it is quite dirty. I won't go over again all the problems and irritations that were currently befalling our citizens, and I can't say that in future that they would diminish.

What I can say, though, is that the people of this nation were not focusing on all the failings that they could see round them. They were instead working hard to construct new lives for themselves and their families. They were just starting a magnificent Baby Boom that would see this nation having greater freedom and greater prosperity than **their pre-war parents could ever have dreamed of.** And they did it in this our protected and insular world for a period, of seventy years, that hopefully will last forever.

So, I say to you, if you were born in 1945, and if you can forget some of the hardships you have doubtless suffered, then you should join together with the other lucky ones and rejoice in being born into this nation and, specifically, being born into this nation **in 1945.**

COMMENTS FROM READERS

Tom Grahame, Spears Point.....Some history writers make the mistake of trying to boost their authority by including graphs and charts all over the place. You on the other hand get a much better effect by saying things like "he made a pile". Or "every one worked hours longer that they should have, and felt like death warmed up at the end of the shift." I have seen other writers waste two pages of statistics painting the same picture as you did in a few words....

Barry Elliott, Balgownie....you know that I am being facetious when I say that I wish the war had gone on for years longer so that you would have written more books about it...

Edna College, Auburn.... A few times I stopped and sobbed as you brought memories of the postman delivering letters, and the dread that ordinary people felt as he neared. How you captured those feelings yet kept your coverage from becoming maudlin or bogged down is a wonder to me....

Betty Kelly, Wagga Wagga....Every time you seem to be getting serious, you throw in a phrase or memory that lightens up the mood. In particular, in the war when you were describing the terrible carnage of Russian troops, you ended with a ten- line description of how aggrieved you felt, and ended it with "apart from that, things are pretty good here". For me, it turned the unbearable into the bearable, and I went from feeling morbid and angry back to a normal human being....

Alan Endine, Hornsby. I particularly liked the light-hearted way you described the scenes at the airports as the American high-flying entertainers flew in. I had always seen the crowd behaviour as disgraceful, but your light-hearted description f it made me realise it was in fact harmless and just good fun.

In 1947, Labor was still in power, but would not give motorists much petrol until 1950. The Poms were firing rockets over our Aborigines, while Menzies was discovering Reds under our Beds. Our new Governor General was not a Pom, but a local lad, and Princess Elizabeth said yes to a Greek. Six boys under 17 were gaoled for life for rape, and 10 o'clock closing might stop the six o'clock swill. Indonesia, India and Israel wanted the colonials to go, and cricket was again thriving on on-field hatred of the Poms. Most of our foreign travel was still done by great big overseas liners. These were striking times.

In 1948, there was no shortage of rationing and regulation, as the Labor government tried to convince voters that war-time restrictions should stay. The concept of free medicine was introduced, but doctors (still controlled from Britain) would not co-operate, so that medicines on the cheap were scarcely available to the public. Immigration Minister Calwell was staunchly supporting our White Australia Policy, though he would generously allow five coloured immigrants from each Asian nation to settle here every year. Burials on Saturday were banned. Rowers in Oxford were given whale steak to beat meat rationing.

In 1967, postcodes were introduced, and you could pay your debts with a new five-dollar note. You could talk-back on radio, about a brand new ABS show called "This Day Tonight." . Getting a job was easy with unemployment at 1.8 % – better that the 5% 50 years later. Arthur Calwell left at last. Whitlam took his place. Harold Holt drowned.

In 1968, Sydney had its teeth fluoridated, its sobriety tested for alcohol with breathalisers, and its first Kentucky Fried. And it first heart transplant. Demos against the Vietnam War, often violent, were everywhere all the time. The casino in Tasmania was approved. We won a pot of gold at the Olympics, Lionel Rose became the first Aboriginal to become a World Boxing Champion, and poet Dorothea Mackellar died at the age of 82.

****

Chrissi and birthday books for Mum and Dad, Grandma and Pop, and Aunt and Uncle and cousins and family and friends and work and everyone else.

Don't forget a good read and chuckle for yourself.

Born in 1959?
What else happened?
AUSTRALIAN SOCIAL HISTORY

RON WILLIAMS

In 1959, Billy Graham called us to God. Perverts are becoming gay. The Kingsgrove Slasher was getting blanket press coverage. Tea, not coffee, was still the housewife's friend. Clergy were betting against the opening of TABs. Errol, a Tasmanian devil, died. So too did Jack Davey. There are three ways to kill a snake. Aromarama is coming to your cinema.

****

AVAILABLE AT ALL GOOD BOOK STORES AND NEWS AGENTS